*For the millions (soon to be billions) of people
seeking meanings in their inner sounds.*

The Ringing Sound

Conscious Living Press, LLC
P.O. Box 50593
Austin, Texas 78763-0593
www.ConsciousLivingPress.com

ISBN: 0-9665358-0-4

First Edition Paperback
1 2 3 4 5 6 7 8 9 10

Manufactured in the United States of America

The Ringing Sound

an Introduction to the Sound Current

By
Eric Gustafson

Conscious Living Press, LLC

www.ConsciousLivingPress.com

Many special thanks

To the following people:

My Partner
Sharrin Michael

My friends at Conscious Living Press
Michele LeBien and Joseph Schultz

Our Editor
Christina Murray

For their wonderful support and suggestions
Chet Braun, Ellen Coleman, Michael LaVigna
and Bryan Mitchell

Great Thanks also to the authors quoted
within for bringing their knowledge forward.
I suggest reading as many of these books as possible.
You can find a complete listing in the Resource Guide
near the end of this book.

Contents

CONTENTS

Illustrations

Forward

Do You Hear a Ringing in Your Ears ?

If you said yes, you are not alone. Millions and millions of people have sought medical advice hoping to find an answer to the ringing in their ears, only to find there is little or nothing that medical science can do for them. They are told they suffer from tinnitus or similar maladies. Many of these diseases and their causes are not even well understood by modern medicine.

Although these buzzing, ringing, rushing sounds have been given new names by medical science, they are not new. They are perhaps as old as humankind. In times past, a great deal was written and taught about how to use these sounds productively. Techniques associated with inner sounds involve the development of internal energy or what may be called spiritual power. Modern practitioners of such techniques often refer to these sounds as the sound current. Studying the sound current is an ancient science and the topic of this book.

Although this book may be regarded as an alternative discussion of tinnitus-like symptoms, it is not intended to replace or offer medical advice. It should only be viewed as an adjunct to orthodox medical or psychological solutions. The intent of this book is merely to offer the insights of ancient practices on a topic that seems to baffle contemporary people. These practices have been beneficial to many individuals by helping them come to better terms with their phantom sounds.

Sound current techniques also hold great potential for the expansion of consciousness. To reach into the sound current's mysteries is to begin a personal adventure of self-discovery.

Enjoy !

This sound is the source of all manifestation.... The knower of the mystery of the sound knows the mystery of the whole universe.

— Sufi Hazrat Inayat Khan

As recorded by
— Joachim-Ernst Berendt
*The World Is Sound:
Nada Brahma*
p. 38

Introduction

What Is The Ringing In My Ears ?

This book is an introduction to the audible life stream, or sound current, and sound current techniques. This current of sound is within each of us. While most people do not become consciously aware of its presence, many do. Some have even sought to comprehend its true meaning.

Explanations always call for deep thought. But when you actually dream, be as light as a feather.

— Carlos Castaneda
The Art Of Dreaming
p. 22

The sound current is an ancient topic. It has been known by many names in different communities throughout the world. Sustained cognition of the sound current has long been a goal of many secretive spiritual schools. The students in these schools study techniques that allow them to access the energy within the sound current. This energy is normally first heralded by a ringing sound having no apparent source in common reality.

Spontaneous Development

Seekers of the sound current are not the only ones who encounter it. Conscious awareness of the sound current can be spontaneous and can appear for no apparent outward reason. I routinely meet untrained people who are keenly aware of the sound current. The responses of these people vary as much as the sounds they hear. Some think it is intriguing. Some find it weird or annoying. Others are frightened.

My Purpose

The purpose of this book is to address these concerns by bringing knowledge of the sound current to light. A major step in alleviating personal fears surrounding phantom sounds may be to realize that sound current practitioners regard the phantom sounds associated with the sound current as natural phenomena. These are seen as manifestations of an energy flow that can be perceived as sound, hence the name: "sound current." This name is derived from our <u>interpretation</u> of the energy as sound. The sound current typically first manifests as a ringing sound in the right ear.

Disclaimer

No medical advice is being offered. This book does not purport to convey any medical advice concerning the causes of tinnitus and other biological disorders reputedly producing similar side effects. This book is intended to be a philosophical or spiritual exploration of a condition that may have serious corresponding medical implications for certain people. Any medical concerns should be directed to your doctor or healthcare practitioner. The intent here is simply to make information available regarding practices used for centuries to cultivate personal vitality from the energy source known as the sound current.

About This Book

The idea is simple but bold: to introduce all of the main aspects of a far-reaching esoteric subject in a practical, meaningful and concise way. First, the personal experiences of several individuals will be shared allowing you to make comparisons to your own encounters with this most amazing phenomenon.

My goal is to cover both the subjective and objective aspects of the sound current experience. To facilitate that goal the nature of perception in general, and the perception of the sound current more specifically, will be analyzed. The insights of modern science will also be applied to our topic. Basic questions regarding the nature of energy will be considered. With all of this information, a practical discussion will offer possible conclusions about the true nature of the sound current. Last, a brief history of sound current studies and some "how to" instructions will be given for those who are intrigued.

The Title

Coming up with a title that covers all the aspects of this book has been a tough job. My original title used the phrase "audible life stream" to convey both the practical and *spiritual* essences of the subject. To me, the word "audible" describes the very real and perceivable aspect of the sound current. "Life stream" refers to its vital essence. In some spiritual schools, the sound current is regarded as the Life Stream of Creation.

Spiritual here refers to energies outside of the realms of acknowledged perception.

Like this book, the sound current has been given many names, reflecting its complex nature. In the end, I chose the current title because it speaks directly to those for whom it was intended. This is a book for people who perceive unusual sounds and want to know more about them.

The Term "Sound Current"

Throughout this book the term "sound current" is used because it has no theological overtones. The study of sound current energy need not offend any *religion*. Done well, it should assist in clarifying personal beliefs. Issues will be explored without religious bias. Any religious context in which an individual chooses to frame the information is a purely personal matter. I am personally interested in the mystic roots of all religions. I consider myself a very practical, spiritual mystic. I live and study

The word **religion** originates from the Latin religio or leig which means to tie fast or bind [to Higher Truth].

19

the nature of reality through the art and science of energy awareness.

I have tried to achieve a balance by providing something for both the highly practical and the esoteric reader. The hope is that the practical, empirical reader is free to approach the topic in a straightforward manner without being troubled by the esoteric seeds embedded in the rational dialogue. It is also hoped that those readers interested in what might be considered the more spiritual aspects will find most of their questions answered.

There are dramatic opportunities for personal evolution in the sound current. However, insofar as is possible, the discussion will remain empirical, or at the very least anecdotal. The really way-out philosophical issues are primarily relegated to the last chapters. But even these more abstract statements reflect my own personal experience. Nothing is stated in these pages that I have not personally confirmed. Real mysticism may begin in faith but it should be confirmed by experience. In that spirit, this is a completely practical introduction to the sound current.

This is a practical approach to what many consider the most profound energy in the Cosmos. It is a reflection of my own pragmatic background, which includes a degree in physics. Even my esoteric training has, for the most part, come through very practical teachers. My sound current teacher, for example, was a very grounded and analytical individual. Decades of various internal martial arts and extreme meditation practices seem to have only contributed to my pragmatic approach to energy.

In short, I have pursued knowledge through two avenues, science and mysticism, until both converged into one path. This path has allowed me to experience the mystic's world while retaining my objectivity in everyday life. As a result, I do not proceed on faith alone and do not expect you to either.

Most of the information given in this book will have sources referenced. The anecdotal stories are drawn from first hand experiences. For those so inclined, the mystic aspects of the sound current are also introduced.

Sidebar Column

The *sidebar column* of each page will be used for referencing sources, giving new definitions, and providing intriguing tidbits and illustrations. Each time a new word appears, it is written in *italics* and its definition appears in the sidebar column. For those of you who do not want to miss the magic in life, the sidebars are also sprinkled with esoteric quotes. The references and quotations from current literature are also meant to serve as a resource list of suggested reading.

Exercises

Exercises are provided throughout the book. Chapter Ten is a "how to" lesson in sound current meditation techniques. Practical experience is the best teacher. You should be relaxed and comfortable while performing these exercises. Never perform any exercise that may alter your state of consciousness when your normal clear and present conscious awareness is required for safety. For example, do not practice any of the exercises in this book while driving a car.

Sidebar

This column will contain source references and miscellaneous tidbits. For specific information on publishers, see the detailed Resource Guide in the back of the book.

Resource Guide

A complete bibliography can be found at the back of the book.

Index

An index is provided near the back of the book for quickly looking up subjects or definitions by topic, author or keyword.

*I could hear the great humming,
pulsating sound that seemed to
fill all the heavens, the sound of
tremendous energies in motion.*

— Norman Paulsen
*The Christ Consciousness:
The Pure Self Within You*
p. 14

CHAPTER ONE

Sound Current

An Overview

Millions of people are seeking help in their quest to understand what is widely considered a medical malady. Millions more hear sounds they cannot explain, but keep their experiences more or less to themselves. This epidemic of *auditory hallucinations* may have an alternative explanation lying totally outside the normal lines of speculation. This phenomenon is at once complex and yet perfectly simple. Its complexity is demonstrated by western medicine's inability to pinpoint its causes. Its simplicity stems from its direct connection to our basic human nature.

One of the main difficulties in explaining the sound current lies in our western thought processes, or more specifically, in our views about objective and subjective reality. The beauty of our current times is that western science and thought have turned a remarkable corner. What would have been a difficult philosophical argument a few years ago can now be rendered into a pragmatic discussion.

Recent changes in our thought processes allow us to perceive ourselves with greater clarity. Perhaps it is more accurate to say, we can now scrutinize ourselves as beings of perception. We can analyze the act of perception itself in a modern, logical manner.

This is possible because science has come full circle. The art of scientific observation has advanced to the point where it is compelled to investigate and quantify the relationship between the observer and the observed. Modern science now makes

Auditory Hallucination

I use this term not so much to imply "false or distorted perception" as unexplained perception.

Tinnitus

...ringing in the ears that affects about 50 million Americans.... An estimated 12 million Americans have it bad enough to seek medical help...

— Austin American-Statesman

definitive statements about the act of perception. It relates how that act connects the perceiver and the perceived.

Perception is no longer seen as a passive function. The act of perceiving directly affects what is being perceived. No object or event is truly isolated. We are bound up in a totally interconnected, holistic universe. This is one of the fundamental concepts of current scientific thought, but similar ideas have long been expressed by eastern philosophies.

East Meets West

In recent years, eastern thought has flooded into the western cultural awareness. Even as science has come full circle through its meticulous process of trial and error, we in the western cultures have become widely exposed to the dualistic, paradoxical concepts of the east.

Western thought has embraced the ideas of objective and subjective realities. These concepts have become woven into the mainstream of our modern society. Terms like conscious and subconscious have replaced older, more superstitious ones, casting new light on our inner demons.

Jung and others infused modern vocabulary with words that elucidate eastern concepts of subjective reality. We use these terms daily to describe ourselves as beings of perception. These new analytical terms of modern psychology express some of the feelings in bygone concepts of magic and resonate with the intuitive imagination.

Even physicists, our paragons of rationalism, now sound like mystics. They speak of "uncertainty principles," "deterministic chaos" and the "origins of time." Western culture squeezed the magic out of life with microscopes and mathematics.

Now it has found it again in the enigmatic formulas of quantum mechanics and in the deeper nature of the human psyche as it has been revealed and expressed by modern psychology.

Entering the Sound Current

One of the side effects of the modern human condition, which is particularly illuminated and exacerbated by our evolution of thought, is poignantly expressed in our current topic. The perception of phantom sounds on an epidemic scale is more than a reflection of the current overwhelming press of humanity upon itself and the many tensions of our times.

In our modern scientific quest, we have unknowingly driven ourselves to the brink of self-discovery. We are at the thresholds of perception. We have arrived at the voice of creation, as have mystics before us throughout the millennia. Our western path to enlightenment has been one of rational discovery. Now we have only to integrate our *linear* reasoning with the *nonlinear* reality around us. We must incorporate our knowledge into the total picture of ourselves as beings of awareness. This will require an intuitive, holistic thought process.

The key to this adventure is already in our possession. It is the ringing sounds at the edge of our perception. It is called the sound current.

A Brief Definition

Because the study of the sound current is not a well-known subject, the experience of it is often misinterpreted. Let us begin to remedy this situation with a brief definition. This definition will be a little esoteric due to the profound nature of

Full Circle

We shall not cease from exploration. And the end of all our exploring will be to arrive where we started and know the place for the first time.

— T. S. Eliot

Linear refers to a straight line. Linear thinking is straight line thinking where only the big, obvious facts from the past determine a situation's outcome.

Nonlinear processes are greatly influenced by small details. A chance encounter with a stranger can alter the destiny of your life. Scientists "pretend" that events in life are linear for mathematical simplicity, but everything is ultimately nonlinear.

our topic. As we explore the facts in greater detail, we will obtain the foundation required to forge more concrete statements.

Some argue that the sound current's profound implications make it a most elusive topic. I say that the challenges encountered in discussing the sound current lie, not in its elusiveness, but in its all-pervading nature. In a way, we are up against the age-old problem, which many before us have confronted, of defining the nature of existence.

However, we are not trying to engage in a totally philosophical debate. We are seeking pragmatic explanations. To do that, we must develop a common vocabulary. It will take some effort to accomplish that task. Step by step we will construct a more complete view of the nature of the sound current. In the interim, consider this brief definition:

The sound current is an omnipresent energy field that can be directly perceived as sound.

A Scientific Precedent

The idea of an omnipresent energy field permeating the universe may sound odd at first. Some might see such an idea as bordering on the supernatural. In fact, the idea regarding the existence of such an energy field in the physical universe is firmly rooted in modern scientific principles.

Serendipity is the synchronicity of being in the right place at the right time to make a discovery. To some these events are fortunate accidents, to others they are magic.

There is low-level microwave radiation emanating from all directions in the universe. It is viewed as remnant radiation of the big bang, the origin of the universe. Scientists refer to it as the *universal* or *cosmic background radiation*. This discovery earned two scientists Nobel Prizes, but finding the cosmic background radiation was a *serendipitous* accident.

The idea that an omnipresent, unidirectional energy field exists everywhere in the universe was so foreign to those scientists who discovered it that it did not immediately occur to them what they had found. They spent months looking for defects in their equipment that could explain the omnipresent buzz. They even roused nesting pigeons out of their antenna. Eventually, they had to consider the fantastic possibility that the energy field was real.

Anyone who, on first hearing, doubts the presence of an omnipresent, detectable energy field called the sound current is in good company — Nobel Prize winners in fact. But the highly analogous universal background radiation has been observed and measured scientifically. That is not to say that this field of microwave radiation is the sound current; but both are said to relate to the creation of the universe. Both are considered echoes of an omnipresent energy field.

Sound current, as it flows through the human body, has not yet been so scientifically scrutinized as the cosmic background radiation. It has, however, been intensely studied for millennia by secretive spiritual groups.

New Frontiers

Often, as in the case of the cosmic background radiation, discoveries are partly accidental and the initial data require a new *paradigm* before a correct interpretation can be made. The detection of a buzzing sound that seems to be everywhere may be a great discovery for each of us as independent explorers of our personal universes. We should not discount our equipment merely because it is biological and not everyone hears what we hear.

Cosmic Background Radiation

In 1965, Robert Wilson and Arno Penzias, with their horn-reflector antenna at Bell Laboratories, discovered a persistent cosmic noise. They detected low level microwave radiation emanating from all directions in the universe. It turned out to be the remnant radiation of the origin of the universe.

Paradigm shifts involve changing the underlying concepts we use to model our personal realities. Scientists must continually cycle through this process as they uncover new data that simply cannot be explained by their old theories.

Perhaps we are making the serendipitous discovery of a cosmic energy field at the edge of human perception. We should spend more time studying the phenomenon and less time looking for pigeons in our equipment.

What Does It Sound Like ?

The auditory perceptions we have been referring to may be perceived in many ways. Commonly, they take the form of ringing sounds. They may be perceived as anything from a ringing, or a buzzing (like the sound of a florescent light), to music. A common analogy likens the experience to that of listening to high-tension electric power lines. Anyone who has stood near one of those colossal Erector Set-style metal towers with suspended power lines, especially when the air is moist, knows that crackly hissing noise.

Please do not be discouraged if you do not relate to the current descriptions. Just because you do not see an exact description of what you hear does not mean that you are not dealing with the sound current. Many other descriptions will follow and still only relatively few of the possible manifestations of the sound current will be explicitly described. To augment these specific descriptions, I will also categorize general types of experiences associated with the sound current.

Generally, the "sounds" are first noticed in the right ear, but may be detected anywhere. As we will eventually see, these "sounds" are not sounds at all. The sound current is energy passing through an energy channel near the ear. It is only interpreted as sound. We will go into more detail about this when we look at the nature of the sound current and its relationship to human anatomy. For now, the best method for describing the various ways in which the sound current may be perceived is to catalog them and give some examples.

This first list is from a classic yoga book. It describes some of the more common ways in which the sound current may be perceived. Each description is preceded by its *Sanskrit* name.

1. *Cin nadam:* Like the hum of the honey-intoxicated bees; idling engine vibration; rainfall; whistling sounds; high frequency sound.

2. *Cincin nadam:* Waterfall, roaring of an ocean.

3. *Ghanta nadam:* Sound of a bell ringing.

4. *Sankha nadam:* Sound of a conch shell.

5. *Tantri vina:* Nasal sound, humming sound like that of a wire string instrument.

6. *Tala nadam:* Sound of a small tight drum.

7. *Venu nadam:* Sound of a flute.

8. *Mridamga:* Sound of a big brass drum.

9. *Bheri nadam:* Echoing sound.

10. *Megha nadam:* Roll of distant thunder.

Sanskrit is the classical old literary language of India as cultivated from the third century BC. It is associated with the descriptive analysis of Hindu religious texts. Its value lies in its lexicon of highly evolved intuitive energy descriptions. It is one of a few ancient languages which reputedly expresses the essences or primal sounds of individual objects and concepts.

List quoted from:

— Rammurti S. Mishra, M.D. (Shri Brahmananda Sarasvati)

Fundamentals Of Yoga:

A Handbook of Theory, Practice, and Application

p.135

Additional common descriptions would include the chirping of a cricket(s) or a boiling teakettle whistling. Flowing water or wind are also common descriptions. These sounds can be of a high frequency, like a florescent or halogen light, or of a very low frequency with an undulating or even slowly oscillating palpable physical quality. They can be smooth and harmonious, or very rough and jangly. They may be barely audible or seem almost deafening. Often these tones appear just at the edge of hearing or sound very distant. When they seem close and loud, they can actually vibrate the physical body.

When Would I Hear It ?

The sound current is most noticeable during periods of high stress or, paradoxically, deep relaxation. It may be fair to say that perception of the sound current is most notable when the body's *homeostasis* is either highly threatened or highly attuned. Perception of the sound current may be particularly strong under the following circumstances:

- Sleep Deprivation

- Illness or High Fever

- Influence of Drugs or Alcohol

- Physical or Emotional Trauma

Homeostasis refers to the body's natural energy balance (i.e., temperature, chemical and energy) with its environment. Western medicine tends to see our bodies as isolated mechanisms rather than as integrated, synergistic systems, but in spiritual energy practices bodies should be viewed holistically. Everything is connected. Every part affects the whole.

All of the above bulleted items relate to altered states of consciousness. They also represent potentially dangerous situations for the physical body. None of these is advised for inducing perception of the sound current. Aside from the obvious dangers of employing such methods, there is an inherent distortion of the natural experience associated with the stress created by such methods. Consequently, the psyche cannot interpret the resulting perceptions well. The quality of subsequent experiences is also compromised by the body's attempt to recover from the onslaught of imbalanced energy.

Positive Practices

The sound current can be explored in its positive aspects through quiet inner stillness or focused energy techniques. The following practices are recommended for enhancing perception of the sound current and personal vitality in general:

· Deep Relaxation Techniques

Example: Yoga

Yoga refers to the integration of intellectual learning into practical personal experience. Traditional yoga postures and exercises foster relaxation and vital energy. The combination of these seemingly opposing effects can produce ecstatic states.

· Certain Types of Breathwork

Examples: Rebirthing, Holotropic Breathwork

Rebirthing and Holotropic Breathwork are specific practices that cycle breath effectively. This facilitates the body's natural progression towards increasingly higher levels of homeostasis. These practices may promote physical and emotional clearings that are often accompanied by profoundly altered states of awareness.

Yoga is the Sanskrit word meaning to yoke. The concept is similar to the word religion, which means to bind [to God]. Both terms imply a bonding of one's earthly experience with a higher level of existence, or what may be referred to as a spiritual experience.

Rebirthing

The purpose of rebirthing is to remember and re-experience one's birth; to relive physiologically, psychologically, and spiritually the moment of one's first breath and release the trauma of it.

— Leonard Orr and
Sondra Ray
Rebirthing In The New Age
p. 71

· Certain Types of Meditation Practices

Example: *Surat Shabda Yoga*

This is an ancient spiritual practice that seeks to align the practitioner with the Source of Creation through communion with the sound current.

It should be noted that children are often naturally attuned to the sound current, much as they are with many other spiritual things. Adults disregard it, so eventually most young people follow their example and learn to ignore it as well. It would be interesting to live in a culture where children were allowed to grow up with the sound current.

Other Possible Physical Sensations

In addition to auditory perceptions, there are several related physical sensations that can accompany the sound current. These would include:

· Fizzing

This is similar to static electricity on your skin, like the kind caused by a wool sweater when the humidity is low or by clothes just out of the dryer.

· Vibrating

This is energy running in the body. It feels like mild electric current.

· Tetany

This is an exaggerated version of the fizzing and vibrating. Numbness, cramping and pain may accompany it. If you have experienced tetany, contact a Rebirthing coach to learn how to control the energy with breathwork.

· Pressure Over the Ears

This feels like the sensation of taking off in an airplane or as if someone has cupped her hands over your ears, but there is usually no sensation of actually being touched. Outer sounds may be muffled along with the sense of pressure.

· Tunnel Vision

Peripheral vision may disappear. The sensation is that of looking through a tunnel. There may be an accompanying feeling of movement through the tunnel. The "walls" of the tunnel may appear dark or seem to be made of light or banded light that can streak by with apparent motion.

· Visual Hallucinations

Close contact with the sound current can completely alter one's state of awareness. You may see sounds as light or enter into a visionary state. Experienced guidance is advisable in these "mystical" encounters, but be aware that you possess your own inner guide.

Dramatic Symptoms In Altered States

As he talked, I began to feel a strange pressure; it was a physical heaviness. My eyes teared to the point that I could hardly make the shape of the furniture. My vision seemed to be totally out of focus....There were streaks of chartreuse phosphorescence that illuminated dark, moving clouds. Then, as abruptly as it had faded away, my eyesight returned.

— Carlos Castaneda
The Fire From Within
p. 116

The Extraordinary

Because perception of the sound current feeds the mechanism of perception itself, extraordinary experiences may occur. It is for this reason that techniques for perceiving the sound current have, in the past, been guarded by mystery schools. These secret practices were shown only to specially prepared "initiates" or devotional students.

While these schools can be very helpful, I see no cosmic imperative to enter into devotional practices in order to study the sound current. Everyone has access to the sound current. I feel that everyone instinctively understands the sound current, but we allow our fears and desire for control to overwhelm our natural growth.

A flower blooms in its time. Spiritual growth should not be dictated. Each of us needs to discover his or her inner truth and spiritual powers. In spiritual matters, we need to learn to relax and listen to our innermost feelings.

This is especially true in the case of fear. Though fear is a natural response to the unknown, it can prevent us from passing through gateways to our own evolution. This is often the situation people find themselves stuck in when it comes to the extraordinary sensations accompanying the sound current.

Do not be afraid of the sound. Be prepared to step into the extraordinary. If you need help, ask for it. If you ask, it will manifest.

The Time Is Now !

These amazing sensations are merely further testimony to the complexity of our human state of existence. Anyone who is doing personal energy work, metaphysical work, esoteric martial arts or specialized activities such as yoga may experience some or all of these effects.

Spontaneous Development

Conscious awareness of the sound current can be spontaneous and appear for no apparent outward reason. Such incursions are sometimes referred to in mystic circles as "receiving the knock of Spirit." Uninvited episodes can be very disturbing, particularly to those who do not understand the nature of what is occurring.

This is not to say that people who have accidentally induced these symptoms have made a mistake. Quite the contrary; they may have done well indeed. These sensations may be indicators of enhanced personal energy that can foster greater vitality and awareness. The key is to follow a natural path of development. Proper techniques can facilitate this personal growth.

Simply be aware that the onset of the sound current is usually a sign of change. It may be inviting you on a new direction in your personal journey.

Perceiving The Sound Current

As mentioned earlier, the most common place to first notice the sound current is in the right ear. Once you give up the idea that this is a sound that you <u>hear</u> in the normal way,

Change Is Movement

Change is energy in motion. Any time you are undergoing intense personal change, you are more likely to become conscious of the sound current and experience its "symptoms." More importantly, when you become conscious of the sound current you are going to experience intense personal change. Going through the growth process is more rewarding and less work than trying to avoid it.

you may be surprised to find that the actual location of the sound current might not be directly in your ear. The sound current frequently resides slightly above and behind the right ear. Another common place is located one or two inches below the crown, or hair swirl, of the head. This position is just above the first location. The left side of the head has the same two points. These four skull points along with the crown point are the most common places for beginners to perceive the sound current.

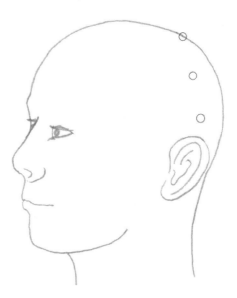

Illustration Of The Head
These are common contact points for the sound current.

If the body is stressed, sound current may be flowing from these skull points down through the neck. This energy may flow into any portion of the body. It may even be sensed outside the physical body. Those who have not experienced this may wonder how you can "hear" sounds other than with your ears.

While it is not exactly the same, I will offer an analogy. Hearing the sound current somewhere in your body other than in your ears is like hearing your heartbeat when you exercise. You hear the pounding of your heart through the arteries that pass near your ears. Simultaneously, you feel your heart beating in your chest and say, "I can hear my heart beating." In a similar way, we extend our sense of hearing in regard to the sound current. This is one of those sensations which is difficult to describe, but is well-known to anyone who has experienced it. Of course, hearing an internal sound that appears to be completely outside of your body is even more bizarre.

Energy Anatomy

Our energy anatomy extends beyond the physical boundaries of our skin. This is a scientific fact, not new age rhetoric. Our bodies produce many subtle, yet detectable, electromagnetic fields. These fields include microwave, infrared and others.

Martial arts teachers speak of one's dynamic sphere. By that they mean one's ability to detect intruders or potential enemies at a distance without first seeing them. This requires being aware of people around you, and what they are doing, on a new level of consciousness. This can only be understood if we expand our knowledge of how we perceive and analyze through unusual modes of awareness.

Studying modern sciences, such as biophysics, can broaden our insight into how the human body sets up its many measurable electromagnetic fields. There are other energy fields that are perceivable to intuitive individuals but difficult to confirm with current scientific technology.

A *clairvoyant* might say that our immediate personal energy normally extends out about arm's length. It is quite possible to become aware of the sound current vibrating within that aura of personal energy. Even more abstract possibilities exist, but let us save those for later. Right now we are just cataloging phenomena for the benefit of those who may have experienced some of the more unusual expressions of personal energy.

A **clairvoyant** is an individual who can consciously perceive energy fields, especially around living beings, which are not normally apparent. Some clairvoyants can interpret the colors and patterns in these energy auras to detect disease or make other personal prognoses.

Exercise
Hearing the Sound Current

This is a simple exercise to demonstrate that the sound current can be consciously summoned. Sit quietly. Take a deep breath and relax as you slowly exhale through your mouth. Close your eyes and place your thumbs over your ear canals with your forefingers touching above the apex of your head. Take another relaxing breath and listen as if you were trying to hear the faint sounds of a distant waterfall. Sit quietly for a couple of minutes with your ears covered and listen to the inner distant sounds. Intend to hear the sounds and they will come. Notice their depth. The sounds are not flat. Rather, these sounds have dimension. Earplugs also work very well for this.

Perceptual Blocks

There can be bona fide blocks to perceiving the sound current. A guru or teacher can help here — not by giving the sound current to the student, as many would have you believe — but by dealing with the blocks, or helping the person clear their own energy. In these issues, the mere energetic presence of the teacher can be valuable.

Your Energy Environment

Anything in your environment can affect your perception of the sound current. Human beings all have similar energy structures. In that way, we are like tuning forks resonating with each other. Through sympathetic vibration we strongly affect one another's energy climate. Everyone knows what tension, or emotional pressure, in a room full of agitated people feels like. Similarly, we know what attraction between people feels like. These energy connections affect emotional states and change the tone and quality of individual perceptions of the sound current.

People are not the only things that create energy fields. Geographic locations also have unique energy qualities. Large, physically dramatic landscape features (i.e., mountains, canyons, etc.) can also be dramatic energyscapes. These features can affect perception of the sound current.

Forests and flora produce collective energy structures just as groups of people can. Walking between two trees can create a palpable energy shift for people.

Sometimes a small geographic area only a few feet across might shift the tone of your sound current as you pass through it. The reasons for sound current shifts in a particular area are not always readily apparent in the physical world.

Exercise ━━━━━━━━━━━━━━━━━━━━━
Monitoring the Sound Current

As an exercise, if you hear a tone during your daily routine, monitor it as people approach you, or as you take a walk through different areas. Be aware of changes in tone or volume. Notice what is happening around you when the sounds shift. When you become aware of shifts, ask yourself, "What does that mean to me?" You may be surprised at your inner response.

The Story So Far

The sound current is an energy field that can be directly perceived by the human body/mind. Many spiritual schools are devoted to understanding this singular phenomenon. To my knowledge, all schools that are aware of the sound current regard it as the ultimate path to enlightenment.

Paranormal

Beyond the range of normal experience or scientific explanation.

— American Heritage Dictionary

Trauma and intense personal change shift the body's homeostasis. In these altered states of awareness, *paranormal* perception of the sound current is more likely to occur. Personal trauma, extreme excitation, profound relaxation or moments of epiphany can induce perception of the sound current. It is regarded as the direct sensation of the energy of creation and it can be utilized.

The sound current is always present, even when unperceived. When it is perceived, it need not be a negative feature of life. In fact, it tends to create tension only when one struggles to ignore it. Acknowledging the sound current gives rise to understanding. It can then become a great key to the development of personal energy and vitality.

If you blot out sense and sound,
what do you hear?

— Zen Koan

As recorded by
— Joachim-Ernst Berendt
The World Is Sound: Nada Brahma
p. 171

CHAPTER TWO

Sound Current Stories

The Anecdotal Approach

Conscious perception of the sound current is common. Those of you who hear sounds that have no explanation in your physical environment may take heart in these stories.

I have chance meetings quite often with people who hear inexplicable sounds. Spiritual students, and persons undergoing life transitions in particular, can suffer many symptoms. Shifts in personal energy can create energy surpluses or imbalances. One of the most frequent results of such an energy shift is the perception of phantom sounds.

It is commonplace for me to have conversations with yoga, meditation and esoteric martial arts practitioners about the various sounds they hear. These conversations usually begin as discussions about their energy exercises then evolve into questions about what they consider to be the peculiar side effects accompanying their practices.

Students of these arts need to realize that they are engaged in energy exercises that were originally designed to heighten awareness. Heightened awareness automatically leads to direct encounters with energies outside of normal perception. Such encounters may be classified as spiritual or mystic experiences.

This phenomenon is by no means limited to spiritual students. I have had impromptu conversations about the sound current with perfect strangers in such places as waiting in line to buy movie tickets and at grocery store checkout counters.

Spiritual Growth

Spiritual students are always in transition. Change is a condition of growth and spiritual practices are a quest for personal growth. These practices can produce many unusual conditions and side effects. Some may be very challenging opportunities.

Spiritual Students

I consider everyone in the school of life to be a spiritual student. Some are just more intentional about it than others. Certainly, anyone practicing an energy exercise, such as yoga, is an intentional spiritual student by my definition.

Do You Ever Hear Ringing ?

On one such occasion, I was waiting in line to buy a movie ticket. Two women in front of me seemed to be having a great time. They were talking in a very animated fashion. Suddenly, one of the women announced to her friend that she was hearing a loud ringing in her ear. Her friend replied that the same thing would happen to her periodically. In a good-natured way, they began to speculate about the possible causes of this phenomenon.

I must have been smiling conspicuously, because the woman who was hearing the sound turned and ask me if such a thing ever happened to me. Joining in their enthusiasm, I asked her if the sound was in her right ear. After a moment of introspection, she acquired a puzzled look. She asked how I could know which ear was ringing. Her friend joked that I had a fifty-fifty chance, but I said to them that this was not quite true.

I told them that there is an ancient form of yoga meditation centered on sounds having no source in physical reality. I explained that this obscure branch of yoga claimed direct experiential knowledge of the source of creation through an audible life stream of energy, called the sound current. "That ringing in your ear may be the key to the Cosmos," I said to her. They thought that was very funny and made jokes until they bought their tickets. They seemed quite content with the explanation. Neither of them showed any fear regarding the sounds they were hearing.

People are often satisfied with this level of knowledge. They are glad to know that there is a positive aspect to the presence of the mysterious sounds, but are not interested in delving further into the mystery.

For the woman buying movie tickets, her perception of the sound current was probably brought on by her exuberant exchange with her friend. This is frequently the case. Whenever we are engaged in intense energetic exchanges, the increased energy flow often makes us aware of the sound current. Playing is a great way to increase vitality, or personal energy. This can lead to an impromptu encounter with the sound current.

Something Must Be Wrong !

On another occasion, I was speaking with a young man about martial arts. He suddenly began tapping the right side of his head with the heel of his hand.

"Are you all right?" I asked.

"It's just this loud buzzing in my head," he replied. "Nothing to worry about, it happens all the time," he continued.

I smiled and asked him, "Are you aware that there is a system of meditation which says the sound you are hearing may be the most profound thing in your life?"

"There is nothing more profound about this noise than something being wrong with my head," he retorted irascibly.

This young man was obviously very disturbed by the presence of the sound. He not only took no consolation from my statement, but he also made it clear by his comments and demeanor that he was frightened by the topic. He had no interest in pursuing it. His distress was obvious, but he left no opening for further discussion. I opted to simply smile and return to our previous topic of *Aikido*.

Thinking Makes It So

The moment you think something is "wrong," it becomes uncomfortable.

— Sharrin Michael

Aikido is a Japanese martial art which literally means "the art of harmonizing with energy" or ki. Aikido is definitely an energy exercise that can lead to intense spiritual experiences.

45

This is the unfortunate response of many people. What we do not understand often frightens us, particularly if something manifests which may be considered symptomatic of a health disorder. Dealing with the sound current, on the other hand, usually falls into the "there is nothing to fear but fear itself" category. The peculiar thing about encountering the sound current, as with many threatening things in life, is that it is easier to pass through the experience than to ignore it.

The sound current, in general, cannot be ignored. It is a persistent feature of life, an ever-flowing river of energy. Resisting the sound current temporarily dams it up. This only increases the pressure and volume of the sound. When the dam breaks the resulting stress can be enormous. In extreme situations, a person may actually lose consciousness.

One Person's Curse Is Another's Blessing

I am frequently struck by the fact that many people are tormented by what I have spent years studying and cultivating. I consider the sound current my greatest tool in my spiritual pursuit of knowledge, wisdom and vitality. The difference for me is that I have intentionally pursued esoteric energy practices. It is less alarming to encounter the unusual when you are specifically looking for it.

All sorts of bizarre things can potentially make themselves known on a path of spiritual discovery, and all of life is a spiritual discovery. The sound current is one of those seemingly bizarre surprises. Fortunately, my questing has also generated a great deal of guidance. I have been blessed in my wanderings with many wonderful and timely teachers. The instructions they provided have taken the scary edge away from the symptoms experienced during heightened states of awareness.

When I first began dramatically manifesting the sound current, I was studying with a meditation teacher who, unbeknownst to me at the time, was privy to secret techniques involving the sound current. Through him I was introduced to practices that had been passed down for millennia. Those practices became the primary keys to my pursuit of expanded energetic awareness.

Many people experience symptoms associated with the direct perception of energy without intentionally seeking them. Some accidentally cultivate energy in what they consider normal pursuits of living. Others do so as a result of suffering traumatic events.

It may be argued that merely living in the current times constitutes a traumatic lifestyle. The ambient energy of our times is intense. The worldwide human population is greater than it has ever been. The press of humanity upon itself and the tension of our modern lives create a very challenging personal energy environment. Many people in this time of intense energy are inadvertently put in conscious contact with the sound current. They often first perceive its presence as auditory hallucinations.

For some, fear and a lack of information prevent them from entering into the mysteries that the sound current has to offer. Beauty and wisdom are waiting there for those who dare, but the opportunity is too often allowed to escape. Many individuals are now seeking personal enlightenment on various levels. Some may already have the greatest of all possible gifts readily at hand, but they do not yet see its value. Of course, I am referring to the sound current.

Traumatic Powers

The following quote is by a remarkable man who was struck by lightning. He was pronounced dead and then revived. The experience facilitated the onset of numerous "psychic powers." It is one of many quotes I will offer you as evidence of the link between altered states of reality and the sound current.

This return to my body put me in possession of its pain.... A ringing started in my ears so loud I thought I was in a bell tower.

— Dannion Brinkley
Saved By The Light
p.64

Crossing the Boundary

Awareness of the sound current need not be a persecution. It is a possible indication of a state of *heightened awareness*, which is an altered state of perception. Heightened awareness in general can be quite liberating.

Heightened Awareness is a term used to describe an altered state of consciousness in which one's ability to intuitively perceive is enhanced, but emotional responses are heightened as well. This means that inner peace and well-being must be cultivated in order to remain balanced.

When I began studying martial arts, one of the primary goals was to heighten sensory acuity. An individual with heightened sensory acuity becomes cognizant of subtle sounds, such as another person's breathing. The movement and rhythm of someone's breathing can telegraph information about the manner in which an individual is moving and what his next move will be. You can even determine how someone is moving from the sound of his shoes striking the floor. This is the sensory awareness of the natural predator within us.

As one seeks deeper into this type of sensory acuity, he often discovers that there are additional sounds far beyond the normal range of hearing. Sensory acuity can even be extended into the nonphysical or spiritual realms where phenomena such as the sound current dwell.

You might think this type of detailed sensory information would be superfluous, or even cumbersome, to one's conscious mind. This is not necessarily the case. What is required is a greater field of awareness and a greater mental acuity. Life's magic lies in its subtle hues.

In the context of martial arts, as in the general art of graceful living, it can be of extraordinary value to perceive the fine details of people's intent through their body language and the accompanying movement of their energy. We may no longer live in nature as predators and prey in the classic sense, but we share the capacity for heightened sensory awareness with our animal neighbors. Contrary to overwhelming the mind, when properly exercised the mind's acuity expands into intuitive realms.

Heightened awareness is the key to greater vitality and personal fulfillment. However, these altered states of awareness are, by definition, not normal states of consciousness. Enhanced perception provides information to the mind beyond the average person's expectations. Society has not trained us to deal with these extraordinary situations. Hearing the sound current is an example of paranormal perception.

My Personal Story

I have had a great deal of experience with the sound current throughout my life. Before I received training, I had never been able to attribute any meaning to it. The only significance I could attach to the strange sounds were that they were more intense during certain states of altered consciousness.

By my early thirties I had studied several types of *meditation*. I had left behind professions in both science and business to live, what I considered at the time, a more spiritual life. I started a cabinet shop with a friend, intent on a quieter existence. The theory was that a simpler life leaves more space for spirituality. To this day I can neither confirm nor deny this hypothesis.

Meditation is the science and art of quieting one's internal dialogue (the voice of our programming for day-to-day living) to reveal a greater connection with inner sources of vitality and awareness.

Meeting My Sound Current Teacher

One day after finishing a job, I parked my truck, loaded with tools, outside the Austin public library and went in to hear a lecture. There had been an announcement in the newspaper. The notice simply said, "A Lecture On *Spiritual Engines* by Bruce

Spiritual Engines was a term used by my sound current meditation teacher for man-made spiritual energy machines. These places generate energies not necessarily detectable by current scientific equipment. For example, the Temple of the Sun at Teotihuacan, Mexico is designed to link humans to the sun's spiritual influences.

Avenell," and gave the date and time. It sounded intriguing even though I had no idea what it meant. The lecture was not on meditation. The speaker was an older man, short, rotund, and mostly bald: kind of a Caucasian Buddha type. He had toured many of the world's powerful, ancient archeological sites, including the pyramids of Egypt and pre-Columbian ruins of Mexico and Central America. He referred to these places as "spiritual engines." It was a very esoteric talk about energy. He spoke about the energy of these places and its effect on human states of consciousness.

As a scientist, I was impressed by his natural understanding of energetic phenomena. As a student of many esoteric practices, I recognized the validity of his knowledge. He had specific information about real paranormal events. I considered myself an expert at pigeonholing metaphysical teachers (I now know better). Only a person who had experienced these states of consciousness could speak with such authority. My own experiences confirmed a good deal of what he was saying. What intrigued me the most was his energy. It was somehow concealed. I could not read him the way I could other people.

At the end of the lecture it was mentioned, almost in passing, that he taught meditation. I called him the next day and we arranged to meet at his home. We had a long and pleasant conversation. He told me that his energy was difficult to read because he kept it "spun in." He approached the study of spiritual energy like an engineer. I liked that. It appealed to the scientist in me. Most of our chat was fairly uneventful except for the camaraderie of finding a fellow traveler. I signed up as a student and he gave me his beginning *energy management* and meditation techniques. The sound current was never mentioned.

It would not be long before I would ask the fateful question. In the meantime, I focused on the techniques he had given me. However, each time I sat to meditate, my ears were ringing, especially my right ear. The sounds were growing increasingly louder during my sessions. Within two weeks the sounds threatened to dominate my conscious awareness during meditation. I was curious about the sounds, but I was intellectually engaged in trying to meditate around them.

I soon met again with my new teacher. We discussed the details of my meditations. Suddenly, I remembered the ringing sounds. By now, they not only dominated my meditations but were with me most of the day. They were an ever-present background. Even when I could not actually hear them, they were there, like a pressure somehow climbing up my spine as I exerted a continuous subconscious effort to maintain a normal state of awareness.

"By the way, what are these crazy buzzing noises when I meditate?" I asked. His eyes widened. He asked for a description of what I was hearing. His excitement intrigued me. I told him the sounds were getting extreme. I heard loud chirping crickets and high-pitched, boiling teakettle sounds. Sometimes they were so strong, it seemed like they should deafen me, but they never seemed to impair my ability to hear. He wanted to know exactly how the sounds changed when I was meditating. I told him that the sounds normally got higher in pitch, with finer tones. They also became louder. Sometimes it felt as if the vibrations were physically shaking me.

I knew I was caught up in a conversation that would shake my world-view, but I did not know what the cause of the excitement was. Then, he began asking me to describe qualities of the sounds that I had not thought about. "Where was I hearing

Energy Management is the science and art of cultivating personal energy. Meditation is an exercise in letting go and flowing, but energy management is an exercise in directed perception and control through light intent.

Sound Current Meditation is a meditation practice where one focuses on, or into, inner nonphysical sounds.

them and what was their direction?" The next thing I knew, he was telling me that I was ready for another kind of meditation. I found myself being instructed on what he called "*sound current meditation.*" We were actually engaged in a conversation on how to listen to these crazy sounds in my head. He told me this was the most potent form of meditation available on the planet. I was completely intrigued and yet stupefied. It seemed so unlikely. I went away like a child with a new toy.

My initial response to the sound current, it turns out, is a typical one. We first hear the sounds like a telephone ringing in another room. The ringing begins to enter our consciousness. On some level, we start to get annoyed that no one is answering the phone. Then we try to block it out and go on with our business. It does not occur to most of us that the call is for us.

My Teacher's Story

It turned out that my teacher had been through a similar process himself. In the fifties, he had studied with a man from India. His name was Dr. Bhagat Singh Thind. My teacher studied with Dr. Thind for almost a decade before he asked him about the sound current. Dr. Thind replied that he also heard the sounds, but he thought there was no significance to them. This bothered my teacher. He instinctively knew that the sounds were a critical component of his meditation. "It was the one thing that was always there," he once told me. He just did not know how to use it. He began to look for someone who could explain the sounds.

Eventually, he went to a talk being given by another Easterner visiting in the United States. His name was Sant Kirpal Singh Ji. My teacher was impressed by the talk. He wanted to become a student, but he had one test to give his potential teacher. He approached Kirpal Singh with one question. He asked him, "What is the meaning of the ringing sounds when I meditate?" Kirpal Singh told him it was his connection to higher awareness. He said there were meditation techniques to develop the energy of that signal. At that point, my teacher became a student of Kirpal Singh. He continued his studies with Kirpal Singh for many years. After some years, he became a teacher in Kirpal Singh's system until he came to another critical question. But that is another story.

The Continuing Story

Through these teachers I entered into the stream of the sound current. This scenario of discovery unfolded for me as it has for generations of seekers before me. I look back now, years later, on my first discussion with my teacher about the sound current and I am amazed. After having been through experiences that in some cases are not even describable, I am amazed that I needed someone else to tell me to pick up that annoying phone ringing in the background. It began my biggest adventure. What I find so amazing is that a huge door of perception is open in front of each one of us and we often do not recognize it.

Profound Sound

...so I reached the soundless sound.

— Paul Reps

Zen Flesh, Zen Bones:
A Collection of Zen and
Pre-Zen Writings

p.26

What is the soundof one hand clapping?

— Zen Koan

CHAPTER THREE

Personal Experiences

More Anecdotes and Observations

The sound current is very real and perceivable. Allow me to share a few more personal experiences. This will give you a chance to compare your own experiences and provide us with a common starting point.

My First Time

My earliest recollection of hearing inexplicable "noise" was as a young child, somewhere between the ages of six and eight years old. I was quietly playing on the floor of our family living room. I remember noticing a rather loud buzzing sound. The sound intensified while I was building a make-believe city out of toys. I began looking around. The only other person present was my mother. It was her response that made the incident so poignant.

I looked for the source of the sound. It seemed to be coming from somewhere. Turning my head to locate it did not provide the usual results. I could not hear where the sound was coming from. The buzzing seemed to be everywhere.

I noticed that my mother did not seem to be reacting to the sound. "What is that sound?" I asked.

"What sound?" she replied. Then she had me describe the noise in some detail. When I told her it was pretty loud, she began asking me about headaches and other possible physical symptoms. I soon began to realize that she was not sharing my fascination with the mystery.

About that time she suggested seeing a doctor. That immediately alarmed me. I recanted as fast as possible, terrified by her reaction. I thought there might be something wrong with me. For better or worse, the incident was sufficiently frightening that I do not remember consciously acknowledging the presence of the sound current again for several years.

Common Ground

This is a typical example of how curiosity about an unusual event can be turned into paranoia by the reactions of other people. I find that children normally respond to perceiving the sound current with curiosity. They usually learn to be alarmed from someone else. Even adults frequently take the anomalous audible tones in stride. Most feel an instinctive sense of fascination. They know there is something significant to be found. It is their second-guessing rational minds and the concerns of others that often conjure up the unpleasant scenarios.

Participants in my "Energy and Spiritual Anatomy" and "Meditation" seminars frequently describe their experiences with the sound current. Often they have heard these sounds for years, or even decades. Some have checked out the medical issues. Most say the tones did not diminish their hearing and they were not concerned. Many have played with the sounds, monitored their tones and noted the conditions under which these tones appear and disappear. These reports come from engineers, waitpersons, business people, medical doctors, healers, teachers, lawyers and civil servants — essentially all walks of life.

Once they have acknowledged the sound current, people often remember childhood incidents. However, many people indicate that the sounds have been with them only for the last few years. I attribute this apparent recent increase in occurrences to our changing times. There is an increasing energetic tension in our lives. This creates both stress and opportunity. The entire gambit of humanity is experiencing these and other anomalous events that were previously found only in the domain of *mystics* and physically or emotionally traumatized individuals.

The Random Visitor

Prior to receiving specialized training, the sound current seems to have wandered sporadically in and out of my life. It intensified during certain times and was out of my thoughts completely at others. Some people have quite a different account. They remember a specific period in their lives, or even a specific day, when they began hearing sounds. These people typically cannot recall any previous experiences. Others have heard sounds all of their lives, including early childhood. They simply remember the sound current as something that has always been there.

One engineer gave a specific day, year and time when he first heard the sound current as a young adult. He investigated the medical options and was told he could go through different treatments but would most likely still hear the sounds. The sounds did not bother him if there was no health threat, so he dismissed the need for any possible medical treatments.

He knew there was something to the sounds and turned his methodical nature on the problem. Intrigued, he started playing with his inner sounds and trying to correlate them with personal circumstances or environmental sources. Certain places, he found, always affected the sounds in the same ways. People also affected his sounds. Some people made his sounds louder.

Mystics
The fine line between genius and insanity can be extended to include the fine line between the mystic and the insane.

The task is not of my seeking...making available the knowledge which has come to me in the course of many years' experience of the strange by-ways of the mind which the mystic shares with the lunatic.

— Dion Fortune
Psychic Self-Defense
p. 9

Others seemed to "upset" his sounds. They caused inharmonious tones. He soon realized that he preferred to avoid those who upset his harmonious tones.

When I met this man at one of my seminars, he had already been playing with the sound current for many years. After researching all types of literature and making inquires to other spiritual teachers, he had concluded that no help was available in his quest to understand his mysterious sounds.

It was wonderful to watch him light up as we began discussing the sound current. He was astonished that I knew what he was talking about. Even more amazing to him were the characteristics that I described to him that he had never really noticed. When I commented that strong environmental forces usually create tones in one's left ear, he immediately agreed with me but had never realized that connection before.

It is always a treat for me to see the excitement in people when they are finally able to engage in a meaningful conversation with someone about the sound current. Tremendous relief and enthusiasm are released when they turn from trying to figure out what is wrong with them to finding the real meaning behind the sounds. At that point, they go from hearing random noises to listening to the sound current.

Sudden Appearances

Some people have dramatic introductions to the sound current. It comes on strong and quite suddenly, taking the form of an overpowering experience. Fear is a natural response of the uninitiated in such cases. Information and understanding are the solution.

Barring any possible organic dysfunction, these types of extreme experiences with the sound current may be heralding the onset of psychic experiences of the caliber described by mystics and biblical prophets. It is imperative in such situations to release any outer fears and rely instead on your *Inner Knowing*.

Passing into such an event with impunity requires a clear mental and emotional state to avoid manifesting inner demons. The secret is to always remain calm enough to hear your own still, quiet, inner voice. Be discerning. Do not panic.

Inner Knowing, or Silent Knowledge, is a knowing at the soul level. It is facilitated by the sound current, which is our connection to higher fields of awareness.

My Second Time

After my initial encounter with the sound current as a child, I do not recall having any subsequent encounters until I was sixteen. Lying in bed one evening, after experimenting with cannabis, I began hearing a roaring noise. The sound was similar to that of a distant jet engine. At first, it seemed far away, but the instant I put my attention on the sound it came into my immediate proximity. I could not tell whether I went to it or it came to me. Whichever happened, I perceived that the sound became very close. When the sound was near everything felt otherworldly. This sensation reminded me of standing beside a continuously breaking ocean surf in some unknown world.

I still had a quasi-normal physical perspective. From that perspective, the roaring noise was focused in my head, but not completely restricted to it. I could feel the sound current throughout my body as a vibration. I felt as if it were shifting my body in space somehow. Lying on my back, the sensation was that of rolling backwards into the bed, turning heels over head.

Upon opening my eyes the apparent motion stopped. As soon as my eyes were closed, the sensation began again. While my eyes were open, and reassuring me that my physical body was motionless in bed, little happened. As soon as they were closed, the roaring sound took hold of me again and the backward somersaulting sensation resumed.

Astral travel is the idea that one's consciousness can leave the physical body as energy and travel, perceive, and remember the experience.

At the time, I knew about *astral travel*. I had even experimented with it on several occasions. It occurred to me that I might be leaving my body. However, that did not stop my mounting concern. I could not control the sensations. I was afraid to fall asleep in that condition. The thought crossed my mind that something might be physically wrong with me. I considered the possibility that I was in the process of dying from some sort of brain tumor or something. It was at once scary and intriguing.

I stayed awake and played with the feelings until they subsided, about forty-five minutes later. After the altered state passed, I fell asleep without apparent further incident. I did not know what to make of the whole thing. My mind was put at ease the following morning when I awoke without any symptoms. The memories were dreamy and yet vivid.

I experienced a similar, even more alarming, episode the next time I artificially shifted states of awareness. After that I discontinued any further experimentation with mind-altering substances. Then one night the vibrations resumed unaided, while I was drifting into sleep. This rekindled fears of mortal threats, but I intentionally went further into the experience, trying to enhance the vibrations. Often the results were sensations of traveling, but I could rarely understand or even remember what followed.

I found that the unaided experience felt more natural. I was choosing to participate rather than having the experience happen to me whether I wanted it to or not. Soon, sounds and vibrations began manifesting regularly in my meditations. They would swish me away like a leaf carried off by a river or blown away by a wind. Psychic events and full-blown mystic visions followed.

Encountering the Paranormal

One evening at dusk, I was walking down the street to my family's home, in what I thought was a normal state of awareness. A presence behind me literally made the hair stand up on the back of my neck. I wheeled around to look down the tree-lined road. Something was shaking the two farthest trees at the road's dead end, perhaps two hundred yards away. As I watched, those trees stopped shaking and the next two, closer to me, began.

It seemed like the wind was alive and shivering. The tremor in the air advanced on me, moving the trees one pair at a time, one on each side of the road. After a slow steady progression the distance had been closed. Suddenly, the gust hit me. I almost lost my balance. It held a chill totally out of context with the season. A terror leapt up inside me that I felt had to be suppressed at any cost. The wind seemed to be attacking. I willed myself to a calm and centered place. The commotion died immediately, but I was left stupefied by the confrontation.

As a result of the encounter, I temporarily stopped all of my esoteric pursuits except martial arts. I needed psychological and energetic grounding. My physical and mental condition, which had been superior, decayed. I had tried to cross the oceans of the subconscious in a rowboat. Drugs had unnaturally

Paranormal Wind

At this time of the day, in the twilight, there is no wind. At this time there is only power.

— Carlos Castaneda

*Journey To Ixtlan:
The Lessons of Don Juan*

p. 64

shattered my barriers of perception, unleashing events for which I was unprepared. They opened a door on what Carlos Castaneda and others have referred to as "the easy path," "the dark side of our nature" or "the left-hand path."

The Dark Side

Obi-Wan: [Darth] *Vader was seduced by the dark side of the Force.*

— George Lucas
Star Wars

A two-year struggle to recover my personal well-being ensued. After a year of travel, I entered college at the University of Miami in Florida. Through an acupuncturist I met a Buddhist martial artist. He had been raised in a temple in China. He and a visiting grandmaster from Taiwan taught me Tai Chi, internal energy exercises, breathwork and more meditation techniques. With breathwork and internal energy exercises I re-anchored my energy in the physical world and my health returned.

Tai Chi provided inner calm. I began having mystic experiences again, but this time it was under my own power. It was not forced or distorted. I passed through amazing journeys, but I still never understood the true nature of those experiences until I began studying the sound current.

What Does It All Mean ?

Dreaming Awake

As I was watching a window in a dream, trying to find out if I could catch a glimpse of the scenery outside the room, some windlike force, which I felt as a buzzing in my ears, pulled me through the window to the outside.

— Carlos Castaneda
The Art Of Dreaming
p. 42

Years later, the memories recalled in the stories above, and numerous others, had a great value in my training. When I found my sound current meditation teacher, I acquired a compass enabling me to navigate in the larger Cosmos. I have used that compass to map the pathways to higher awareness, but my life experiences and persistent spiritual pursuits have given me the emotional and mental balance needed to successfully function in those altered states of awareness.

Sleep is an Altered State

It is typical that the sound current tends to manifest during changes in states of consciousness. Often people perceive the sound current during the drift from wakeful consciousness to sleep. For some, the vitality of the tones becomes so acute that it is difficult to fall asleep. Resisting the sound current in such circumstances creates tension and only worsens the situation, like a swimmer who struggles against the river's current. It is much easier to use the energy. Like the swimmer, we must learn to relax into the flow of vitality and use the current's energy.

Spiritual Students

Spiritual students who are specifically seeking altered states can expect to encounter the sound current. The auditory nature of the energy flow within the sound current reveals itself when awareness is shifting to new states. Tone and volume changes indicate new energy configurations.

Perceiving shifts in the sound current is like listening to someone tune a radio from one station to the next. Each station has its own programming format. Each plays a different type of music. In daily life, when one perceives a shift in the sound current, it is typically heralding a change in one's environment or personal energy.

In addition to using the sound current as an indicator of states of personal energy, it can be used to induce specific altered states. Through studying the sound current we can elevate our awareness of energy. States of awareness can be monitored by the qualities of the accompanying sounds. In this way, we can recognize various states of awareness by their respective "feeling tones."

Spiritual Students

My partner Sharrin lived near a public school. On many nights she woke up to what she thought was a school fire alarm test. After trying to track down the source of the ringing sound one night, she realized the ringing was in her head! "I never did figure out what it was until I met you," she told me. She is now an ardent sound current meditator and is no longer at odds with those mysterious sounds.

Exercise
Playing with the Sound Current

Sitting quietly and comfortably with your eyes closed, listen to the sound current's tones. Locate where the tones appear to be within or near your body.

Now isolate a tone on the right side of your head. If one is not there then simply intend to find one. Play with the sound by smoothing its vibrations or raising its pitch by gently reaching into it and intending a harmonious result.

Once you have a nice clean tone, see if you can move it to your crown chakra, or hair swirl. Listen to this crown chakra tone for a few minutes with a quiet mind. Observe yourself and your sound current carefully as you listen.

Changing Tones

In sound current meditation techniques, these sounds may be modulated to produce desired states of conscious awareness. Specific states are associated with certain tones. Knowing a tone allows one to summon a specific related state of awareness.

I am beginning to feel that
Movement in the cells of my
body: it's a movement which is a
kind of eternal vibration, with
no beginning and no end; it's
something from all eternity, for
all eternity (like a sine wave)....

— Mirra Alfassa "Mother"

As quoted by
— Satprem
The Mind Of The Cells
p. 107

CHAPTER FOUR

Not So Rare Experiences

Social Reality

Contrary to popular opinion, many people experience paranormal episodes similar to those previously described as heightened awareness, or altered states of consciousness. A noted psychiatrist, Brian L. Weiss, M.D., author of *Many Lives, Many Masters*, suggests most people have paranormal experiences. In the privacy and sanctity of the client-counselor relationship, many people relate personal tales of paranormal experiences. The rarity of such events appears to be an illusion. The foremost reasons why people do not publicly share such incidences may simply be fear of rejection and a lack of information.

A Frame Of Reference

Most people have no frame of reference to correlate paranormal events with the events of their daily lives. They have been taught a selective reality. The more altered their experiences of reality become, the less likely that they will be able to put these paranormal events into the context of their daily lives.

It is said that sailors and airplane pilots are off course over ninety percent of the time. They must constantly correct their path to remain on a true heading. Our subconscious minds perform a similar feat. Our daily awareness wobbles around its perception of normal reality like a gyroscope guidance system trying to maintain a true course. Most of us do not wander too far off the beaten path, but we are constantly on the fringes.

Commonplace Paranormal

Many told me of their very private experiences of parapsychological events, whether ESP, deja vu, out-of-body experiences, past-life dreams, or others. Many had never even told their spouses about these experiences.

— Brian L. Weiss, M.D.
Many Lives, Many Masters
p.128

Altered states of consciousness can manifest in a variety of ways. They are not always accompanied by dramatic shifts in the perception of reality or visual hallucinations. The healthy mind is quite adept at avoiding situations that are too bizarre for it to comprehend. Many people, however, are cognizant of milder forms of altered reality. One example is the variety of ringing, buzzing sounds I have previously described.

Subconscious Screening

I am suggesting that our lives are much more elaborate than we consciously acknowledge. Our lives are multidimensional. We are continually engaged in systems of reality far outside of anything considered normal. To maintain continuity in our normal physical lives, we screen out unusual information. It is there, but it never reaches our conscious minds.

Just as we are subconsciously privy to our beating hearts, we are subconsciously aware of unusual details in our environment. Normally, most of this more mysterious information is viewed by the mind as background. It rarely passes into our conscious thought.

Social Programming Versus Self Discovery

Social Programming differs from one country to another, but we all inherit the folkways and mores of our native cultures. These customs ensure a stable social environment, but they also limit our worldviews.

Our personal psychologies and our expectations of life motivate our views of reality. We continuously monitor and screen perceptual information in order to assemble our picture of daily reality. But not all of our decisions about the nature of reality are conscious choices. Most of our expectations have been programmed into us through social contact.

The goal of *social programming* is to establish a common reality. This has both benefits and liabilities.

Childhood Programming

We are socially programmed from the beginning. As the previously related childhood story involving my mother and the sound current illustrated, we are given clear directives from those around us, especially our parents, delineating what they consider acceptable behavior and concepts. We learn through the process of socialization what actions will be rewarded and which will meet with disapproval or punishment.

The rewards and punishments may be overt, direct action or covert and quite indirect. Much of the programming we receive is so subtle that it is subliminal. Everyone involved in a given communication continually transfers information on a subconscious level. Social cueing occurs through body language and even subtler mechanisms.

Participants may not be conscious of their role in the cycle of behavior modification. Everyone becomes a programmer even as they are being programmed. We all propagate the system while being more or less unaware of it.

Throughout childhood our personalities develop under the influence of a continual barrage of mostly subconscious approval and disapproval. In this way, we acquire the values of our families, peers and the larger society. That common ground of socially agreed upon reality gives us a meeting place. Our shared languages and systems of interpretation provide a forum where we exchange meaningful thoughts and feelings. But an array of prejudices is embedded in the expectations of those systems. Invisible boundaries are established by social realities that can block the perception of great avenues of discovery. The sound current is one of those avenues.

Committing To Listening

I realized that my listening was so contaminated with judgments and criticisms that I had little free space to hear what the other person was saying.

— Kathlyn Hendricks and Gay Hendricks

The Conscious Heart

p. 53

Expanding Social Reality

Europeans considered the world to be flat until Columbus and Magellan demonstrated that it could be circumnavigated. Until then, the idea that a person could stand on the other side of the world and not fall off was absurd. A round world conflicted with common sense and common experience. In other words, it conflicted with the commonly held reality. Like everyone, early Europeans were limited by the social and scientific realities of their time.

New Horizons

Ferdinand Magellan, in 1519, was the first European to undertake a voyage around the world.

Across the Mediterranean Sea, and almost two thousand years earlier, the story was quite different. In Egypt, it had already been scientifically demonstrated that the world was round. For the *Egyptians* of 300 BC quite a different social reality existed than for their contemporary Europeans. Early Egyptians were not limited by the flat earth concept. Their world was round, as ours is today.

Egyptian Science

Two observations were made at separate locations during an eclipse. The disparate lengths of the shadows cast by objects in these two places proved to those rational investigators that the earth was round. If the shadows were short in one place and at the same time long in another, the surface of the earth had to be curved.

Consensual Reality

Consensual reality predisposes us to not acknowledging certain types of sensory input. Paranormal events such as the sound current are considered rare because we have all been subconsciously programmed to acknowledge only a specific narrow spectrum of reality. Few could argue that early Egyptians had vastly superior intelligence quotients to their European neighbors. Yet, the social programming was so strong that Europeans continued to live on a flat world for nearly two more millennia than the Egyptians. It took some rare individuals to step outside of that enormously limiting perceptual reality and see the earth as a sphere.

In many regards, we are like people under the spell of a stage magician. The magician has hypnotized us and convinced us that the stage does not exist. We cannot see beyond the world described by this magician. The difference is that we have been hypnotized en masse through our own efforts. We are the magicians. We sustain the illusion by our own mutual efforts and determination. We hypnotize each other and ourselves through a sustained system of exchanging limiting information. We mutually agree about what is real and continually reinforce the image of that reality with our entire collective behavior.

Shifting Paradigms

Collective realities are always changing. Europeans woke up one day and the earth was round. Talk about having your world rearranged. Discussions about the possibilities of the sound current seem tame by comparison.

Once a new paradigm becomes part of the collective consciousness, individual achievement on that level becomes more commonplace. Whether it is sailing around the world, breaking the sound barrier, running a mile in under four minutes, or replicating DNA in a laboratory, once the impossible has been achieved, it will be achieved again and again on an ever increasing basis. When a concept is accepted as normal, then it becomes widely demonstrated and acknowledged. This is an illustration, not only of how we limit each other with widely held concepts of reality, but of how we advance each other through our individual and collective progress.

So it is with the sound current. Knowledge of the sound current is on its way to becoming part of the mainstream social reality. As this occurs, new windows of opportunity will begin opening. We must become bold explorers of our own realities.

Breaking Conceptual Barriers

Running a mile in under four minutes was once widely considered humanly impossible. After it was once achieved, numerous athletes were soon able to break the four minute barrier.

Paranormal Events

Whether our subconscious screens out an anomalous episode, or we consciously deny it, the general result is the same. The event goes unacknowledged. People are sometimes frightened by the sound current and similar events that they do not yet understand.

This should not surprise us too much. After all, *paranormal* events are by definition outside the realm of normal life. They do not coincide with common expectations about the reality around us. We have been taught to expect certain cause and effect relationships in our physical environment. When an event occurs which does not reconcile with those expectations we can become puzzled or even alarmed. Such events can threaten our sense of well-being. In our normal context, these paranormal events seem random or otherwise outside of our control.

This is only true because of the limitations imposed by the current mainstream system of expectations that defines our normal reality. These issues can often be clarified through a larger frame of reference. A ship disappearing over the horizon is not difficult to understand if you know the earth is round. Expanding our personal horizons to encompass the unseen energy of the sound current is the challenge we now face.

It is natural that the reach of our perception extends into areas beyond our immediate understanding. That is the nature of our quest for knowledge and of spiritual evolution in general. Each new knowing creates a larger horizon on the unknown. That expanding unknown fuels our search for greater truth as we seek to make it known. It is ultimately an adventure of self-discovery in which the sound current is the principle navigation tool.

Paranormal

"Para" means beyond. So paranormal literally means beyond normal. I think of paranormal events, not as separate from normal reality, but as happenings in a larger domain that includes normal reality. The paranormal aspects of our worlds are simply the unknown, previously uncharted areas.

An Example of Peer Pressure

To move ahead in our explorations, we must see beyond currently held views. As we have seen, paranormal events such as the perception of the sound current are often not discussed due to peer pressure. People who have experiences they cannot explain in normally accepted terms are often afraid of public and peer responses. They simply keep the events private.

An extremely conservative, rational businessman told me about seeing what he thoroughly believed was a flying saucer. He was a young child playing in his backyard at the time. He described the saucer as enormous. It hovered over him for some time. The saucer suddenly accelerated and disappeared in the distance. As a child, he was quite taken by this experience and rushed inside to tell his mother. She immediately rebuked him for lying. His reality was invalidated because it did not coincide with common expectations.

After parental denial of his perception, he only shared the story with a handful of friends over the next twenty-five years. He even went so far as to say that he denies believing in UFOs when publicly confronted with the subject.

What he actually saw is not the issue here. What is important is how he, and many like him, reacted. Many of us simply choose not to share occurrences outside the realm of what we consider socially acceptable. Even when our subconscious does not screen out an abnormal event, we often consciously suppress it for fear of negative social reactions.

What Is Normal ?

Most of the reasons why paranormal occurrences are rarely reported have to do with our preconceptions about what is normal. In a discussion about paranormal activity, most people think of bold miracles. We do not expect the abnormal to subtly creep into our daily lives. Our rational minds are busy framing the events of our lives in standard, contemporary terms. Like the pilot, we are always trying to get back on our normal course.

Events must be outlandish, blatant and prolonged before onlookers take serious conscious notice. The first response to any paranormal event is always to make it normal, to rationalize the circumstances in normal, acceptable terms. We not only deny the big stuff, like UFOs, we even hide our small personal inconsistencies from each other, and eventually ourselves, in our quest to be normal.

The present mainstream system of interpreting reality is too small to accommodate many energetic events such as the sound current. We return to it out of habit and because, until now, it was all we knew. We have been using an inventory list that only included known items and everything else was ignored.

Superstition recognizes a higher order behind the events of our lives and sometimes even recommends courses of action, but it provides no testable explanation or scientific hypothesis to build on.

Until recently science was too primitive to deal with these issues. People relied on *superstitions* to cope with situations outside their scope of so-called normal events. But all this is changing. Perceiving the sound current is no longer a small anomalous happening that can simply pass by unnoticed, like a shadow in one's peripheral vision. Only our own barriers stand in the way of our imminent enlightenment.

First we must break an old habit. When we perceive something striking — a sight or a sound that cannot be rationally explained — then we often jump to what are considered the most obvious conclusions:

1) Something must be wrong with me; or
2) There must be some rational explanation.

The fact that no one can imagine what that rational explanation might be is of little consequence in the struggle for control of one's reality. After all, that is the conclusion most people jump to when another party is relating an impossible tale. It is assumed that the other party did not perceive the circumstances correctly. That individual must be tired, distraught or maybe just plain crazy. Either way, it is presumed that there must be a rational explanation to explain away the apparent paranormal event.

The Rational Explanation

There is indeed always a rational explanation, even in the case of our mysterious sounds, but it may involve unfamiliar concepts. Students of physics experience this all the time in the pursuit of abstract topics such as *quantum mechanics* and *relativity*. Undergraduate students frequently find their common sense in conflict with the reality posited by these theories. People's intuitive experience of nature governs their rational expectations. When the theory of relativity states, "time moves slower for someone moving than it does for a stationary observer," that is profoundly contrary to normal human experience. The fact that it can be demonstrated to be true forces a paradigm shift. One must manually override intuitive perception. I am sure many incredulous early Europeans suffered similar cathartic shifts when it was demonstrated, to the mass consciousness, that the earth is round.

Quantum Mechanics uses information about the energy available in subatomic systems to create probability waves that predict the system's possible future behaviors. Predictions, such as particles materializing on the wrong side of a barrier, often defy common sense but turn out to be true.

Relativity states that everything you perceive is dependent on your frame of reference and relative velocity. There is no absolute time or space.

Absolute, uniform motion cannot be detected.

— *Einstein*

That is why people resist change and why science is both a curse and a blessing. Once someone demonstrates beyond doubt that the impossible is true we call it science. Then we must all reorder our expectations to accommodate the new truth about our reality. Today's magic is tomorrow's science. Nothing could be more magic than the sound current.

Good Data

It often takes years before scientific theory can successfully explain experimental anomalies. Scientists are frequently guilty of throwing out experimental data because it does not show the expected results. Just as scientists are attached to their theories, people are naturally attached to their view of reality. When results do not support expectation, we often throw out the results. The trouble is, the result occurred for some reason. When we perceive an event which deviates from the norm there is usually an opportunity for greater insight right behind it.

Most people who perceive the sound current assume that they are receiving erroneous data. Perhaps our perceptual faculties are more reliable than we think. We should focus on being good observers rather than skilled rationalizers. Maybe the data is good. It may be that our theories and expectations need to evolve before we can come to a more complete understanding of the sounds we perceive.

This is the process of growth and discovery we go through all of our lives. This is the process we are going through in this book. We are expanding our view of reality to include more than what is commonly acknowledged. We are evolving a model of reality based more on the nature of perception and the science of energy than on the fixed view of the material world which is commonly held. In moving from a mechanical view of reality

Absolute Truth

I have noticed that physics professors have a propensity for discussing current theories as absolute laws. This continues in spite of the fact that yesterday's "truths" are constantly revised, upgraded or discarded. Absolute Truth is the Holy Grail. All other truisms are relative to one's frame of reference. Today's rational insight is tomorrow's superstition.

to an energetic interpretation, we are following in the footsteps of both modern physics and mysticism.

Reality Check

The common test for reality is whether other people can corroborate its existence. I have talked with thousands of people about phantom auditory perceptions. Most of the replies I receive to the question, "Do you hear ringing or buzzing noises?" are "yes," "occasionally," "all the time," or "doesn't everyone?" Almost everyone hears the sounds occasionally.

Some may not consider the experiences of the few thousand people I have personally spoken with overwhelming evidence, but it works for me. It is certainly statistically significant when one considers that millions of people in the United States alone are on record as sufferers of auditory hallucinations.

I know from experience that these distressed people are only the tip of the iceberg. Most people never seek medical advice. Of those who do, most never see a specialist. They see their family doctor. Perhaps some drug is prescribed. When the symptoms persist they are told that little can be done. Add this to your own experiences. Talk to your friends. Search your feelings. You will find that there is more going on here than meets the ear, more than just hallucinations.

I submit to you that the sound current is a real phenomenon. It is experienced by everyone to some degree.

While the existence of the sound current is well corroborated by common experience, it has yet to be corroborated

Beyond Sound

All final spiritual reference is to the silence beyond sound. Beyond that sound is the transcendent unknown, the unknowable. It can be spoken of as the great silence, as the void or as the transcendent absolute.

— Joseph Campbell
As edited by
— Betty Sue Flowers
The Power Of Myth
p. 98

by direct scientific measurements made by any instruments other than human beings. Medical science has not acknowledged the issue as anything other than an ailment that is not well understood. But there is a great deal of information that the sciences can contribute to our understanding of the sound current right now.

I have spent years studying the sound current and associated meditation techniques. In writing this book, I have been obliged to refer to the perception of the sound current as auditory "hallucinations." As we shall see, this phenomenon is far more interesting and wonderful than any hallucination.

*You can also learn to manipulate
the subtle layers of the
mind. For that, special
techniques exist, the first of
which is called primordial
sound. It takes its name from
the faint vibrations that can be
detected when the mind is
almost totally quiet.*

— Deepak Chopra
Perfect Health
p. 131

CHAPTER FIVE

Everything Is Energy

The Wisdom of Modern Physics

The vocabulary of modern physics is totally appropriate to the study of the sound current. Both physics and metaphysics endeavor to understand the deeper nature of reality. Metaphysics is an intuitive journey into the forces that lie behind our normal conscious perceptions of life. Physics is the rational study of the forces that motivate physical reality.

Physics has a term for the vital force behind all movement in the physical universe. That term is energy. Energy makes all things possible. This abstract concept of a vitalizing agent lying behind all things is also common in mystical teachings. Both physics and metaphysics may be regarded as the study of energy. Modern physic's gift is the formal expression of this vitalizing agent in highly rational terms.

This chapter explores the insights of modern physics. The bits of rational wisdom uncovered can be applied to our overall understanding of the sound current on both intellectual and intuitive levels.

Understanding the Sound Current

Raw information acquired during a direct experience with the sound current sometime lacks any rational explanation. As thinking beings, we like to clarify our intuitive feelings with intellectual understanding. In this pursuit, we are not seeking to discount personal experiences with the sound current. Instead, we are trying to understand the meaning behind those experiences.

Science Parallels Mysticism

Cosmologists have recently stated that nothing can be known of the physics of the universe before the Big Bang, or act of creation. The same conclusion was recorded by Jewish mystics hundreds of years before.

It could not be recognized at all until a hidden, supernal point shone forth under the impact of the final breaking through.* Beyond this point nothing can be known. Therefore it is called 'reshit,' beginning - the first word by which the universe was created.

" **This primordial point is...the ideal thought of Creation."*

— Gershom Scholem
Zohar: The Book Of Splendor
p. 27

Our goal is not only a plausible scientific explanation of this energy called the sound current, but also a satisfying insight into our personal relationship with it. *Intuitive* feelings can be used to support rational thoughts and vice versa. The object is to play leapfrog with the intuitive feelings formed during direct experiences and the plausible rational explanations for those feelings. Since the sound current lies at the edge of human experience and scientific discovery, we must rally all of our resources to fully comprehend it. By integrating our rational and intuitive sides we are laying the foundations of true wisdom.

Intuition is a knowing which involves subconscious processes, and is therefore sometimes difficult to justify rationally, but often provides great insight.

Science's New Paradigm

We live in a world that is completely altered from the one that existed one century ago. Our modern society is a product of knowing how to rationally and reliably manipulate various forms of energy.

For example, when you turn on your television you are receiving electromagnetic waves that were broadcast from a television station. Those unseen waves fan out and pass through the space around you — unless you are on cable, of course. Your television picks up those traveling waves of information and converts them into coherent pictures and sounds.

Kabbalah is a body of mystical teachings from Jewish rabbis beginning in the thirteenth century. It is comparable to the Hindu Upanishads but has far fewer authors.

Zohar, or The Book of Splendor, is one of the most profound accomplishments of the Kabbalah.

We regard such technology as commonplace, yet it has given us new paradigms of energy and the reality it creates. Science has given us a new vocabulary and increased our range of experience. This larger arena allows us to experience energies that are normally imperceptible in our daily lives. When we switch on the television, we are activating an apparatus designed to receive energies outside of our normal field of perception. Our televisions make those silent, unseen energy waves audible and visible to our physical senses.

Common Miracles

Science has filled our lives with commonplace miracles. Televisions, radios, cellular phones, space exploration and computers have forever altered the way we view reality. During this process of discovery, scientists and the general public have gleaned a great deal of information about how energy behaves. The common person on the street may not understand the finer points of how their television operates, but the average person is very familiar and comfortable with the concept of information traveling through space, cable wires or optical fibers to reach him or her.

Invisible energy carrying complex information would have only been conceivable in mysterious and superstitious terms to our ancestors of only a few generations ago, but we trust in the reality of these silent, unseen messengers. They have become part of our normal lives.

Our intuitive understanding has expanded with our intellectual grasp. Concepts of energy have intellectual meaning and intuitive familiarity. Electric fields, radio waves and a healthy, vital body are all familiar expressions of energy. Someone says, "I feel energized," and we know what that person means. We are now completely comfortable with a reality full of unseen energies.

Now we are on the frontier of another energy revolution. Television signals are proof of the nearby broadcasting station. Gravity testifies to the existence of matter. But, as Shakespeare suggested, heaven and earth abound with even greater mysteries. Just as gravity transmits information about the existence of matter to the physicist, the sound current brings evidence of a greater *Cosmos* to the mystic.

Cosmos

The greater Cosmos includes our known physical universe and many others. It is a unverse of universes.

In my Father's house there are many mansions.

— *Bible: New Testament*
John 14:2

There are more things in heaven and earth, Horatio, than dreamt of in your philosophy.

— Shakespeare
Hamlet, I, v

A Definition

Before we tackle the whole Cosmos, let us begin a little more down to earth. Let us talk about the energy of the physical universe as science sees it. In physics, energy is defined as the capacity to do work. Work is defined in terms of movement. So, we may make the following definition:

Energy is the ability to produce movement.

In science, energy is connected to the ability to produce perceivable, measurable results. When you are driving a car, the energy stored in molecules of gasoline is converted into the movement of the car. Taking energy from gasoline as heat, through internal combustion, to produce motion in a vehicle is what moves you down the highway. But the idea of energy goes much deeper. There are subtler aspects to the science of energy.

It Is All Energy

Einstein showed that everything is energy. In his famous formula equating matter to energy, he demonstrated that physical reality is a manifestation of energy.

$$E = mc^2$$

Speed of Light is 186,000 miles per second. In one year it travels 6,000,000,000,000 miles or one light year.

This equation states that the energy of an object made of matter equals the mass of that object multiplied by the *speed of light*, and then multiplied again by the speed of light. The speed of light is an almost incomprehensibly large number. Multiplying even a tiny quantity of matter times the speed of light twice yields an enormous amount of energy. It takes a lot of energy to make even a tiny amount of matter. The material world is an enormously complex arrangement of inconceivable quantities of energy.

In this vast energy array, all sorts of esoteric energy sources abide, from black holes to dark matter. We have already seen one emission given off by our physical universe: the cosmic background radiation. Are there others? Is the sound current one?

The Big Picture

The most exotic of all sources may be the whole array itself. What kind of energy signal does all of existence radiate? Could it be the sound current? Are we living receptors of the energy signature of existence? If so, are we capable of interpreting such complex energy?

Information Theory

Energy may be understood as information. One branch of physics is called "information theory." Its lexicon incorporates words like *complexity*, *entropy* and *chaos*. These are terms relating to patterns of information.

Think of the material world as a piece of cloth. The threads of the fabric are analogous to objects in the material world. The patterns of the weave are what determine how each thread relates to the others. The weave itself is the information behind the fabric's structure. That information, or energy, determines the final form of the cloth. The weaver's imprinted information patterns the cloth's final reality.

Complexity refers to the levels of order and structure constantly arising in a universe thought to always seek the lowest energy level.

Entropy is a measure of disorder. The higher the entropy of a system, the more disordered it is.

Chaos refers to deterministic patterns that appear in seemingly random systems of energy. Order arises from chaos.

So it is with all structures, including the Cosmos. The echo of the Cosmic Weaver's energy lies behind all things. For students of sound current, the audible life stream, manifesting itself as an infinite variety of sounds and lights, is the Weaver's energy.

Finding Our Way

How strange is seems to say the world is energy. It is stranger still to say that energy is information. We live in the information age in more ways than one. Scientific truths guided us here, but how can we gain a more intuitive understanding of such esoteric thoughts?

We are like the blind men touching the elephant. One feels the rope-like tail, another a tree-like leg, still another the snake-like trunk. Alone these perceptions may be misleading, but together they make a picture. Once one understands the whole elephant, he may grasp how and why it makes its various sounds. In our study of energy, we hope to grasp the meaning of our inner sounds.

Sound And Vibration

…the frequency seemed somewhat below the six-cycle pulsation, perhaps half that rate. Frightened, I stayed with it, trying to remain calm. I could still see the room around me, but could hear little above the roaring sound caused by the vibrations.

— Robert A. Monroe

Journeys Out Of The Body

p. 24

In our studies, we should approach energy more like a diamond than an elephant. Energy has many facets. Each one reflects the world in a new light. The complexity of energy mirrors that of the sound current.

The World Is Vibration

To uncover the nature of the sound current, we first had to conceptually come to the place where we live in a world of energy. We have also seen that energy may be regarded as information. Like mysticism, physics abounds with dualities. In some situations light energy is best described as a wave. Other times it behaves more like a particle, or photon. Sometimes it is useful to see energy as pure information, but there are still other ways to view it.

Energy may be assigned a *frequency*. Frequencies apply to phenomena that repeat themselves. Cyclical events, such as a pendulum swinging, have a frequency that predicts how long it will take a cycle to repeat. If a pendulum is swinging back and forth every second, its frequency is one cycle per second.

Frequency is a measure of the number of times a phenomenon occurs in a certain amount of time.

Systems that continually cycle in this way are often said to vibrate. A vibrating guitar string is similar to an oscillating pendulum in this way. The string cycles back and forth with a characteristic frequency and sends energy through the air to our ears. Information in that vibrational energy means something to us. We perceive it as a particular musical note, or tone.

Exercise
Sound Current Vibes

Consider the vibrational quality of energy. Listen to the sound current for vibrations and modulations. Listen and feel into the subtle nuances of a tone that appeals to you. Send your awareness into one of the spaces between the vibrations.

Different Vibes

Similar to sound, different colors of light have different frequencies. Visible light and audible sound are two types of energy most people can perceive without the aid of any instrument other than their human anatomy, but everything we perceive is a vibrating energy message. Even touch is a vibrating energy message between atoms that we perceive as pressure.

Various kinds of vibrations are present in every physical event. Every level of reality vibrates with its own characteristic frequencies. Light vibrates at one level, sound at another. These different vibrations can coexist in time and space; in the same way, hundreds of conversations can be simultaneously transmitted over one fiber optic telephone line. Sound current has qualities of sound and light.

Exercise ═══════════════════
Seeing the Sound Current

Many people receive light impressions while perceiving the sound current. Close your eyes. Imagine you are inside your head looking at the inside of your forehead, just above and between your eyes. From that place, listen to the sound current and observe. Do not judge. Let your imaging powers loose.

Sympathetic Vibration

The information in energy is transferred through vibrations. A singer vibrates the air with her voice. Those vibrations travel to our ears. Receptors in our ears receive the vibrating energy. These receptors begin vibrating with the singer's voice, in what is called a "*sympathetic vibration*."

Everything resonates to the energy of everything else to some degree, but certain things are well-tuned to receive specific vibrations. When you tune your radio to your favorite station, you are adjusting it to vibrate with the frequency of that radio station's broadcast.

Tuning Forks

Tuning forks are tuned to one note. They will only sympathetically vibrate in unison with that musical note. Place two identically tuned forks close to a third fork tuned to a different note. When the first tuning fork is struck it will begin resonating. Soon the second fork, tuned to the same note, also begins resonating with a sympathetic vibration. The third tuning fork will not absorb enough energy from the dissimilar vibrations to resonate.

When a second tuning fork begins sympathetically vibrating with the energy broadcast by another similar tuning fork, that second vibration is also broadcast into the air. The two forks synchronize with each other as their vibrational modes become locked together. Each becomes a source and a receiver, forming a synergistic system. All sympathetic energy systems, including people, create feedback loops of this type.

Like similar tuning forks, we are tuned to each other and sympathetically vibrate. In this way, we keep each other locked

Sympathetic Vibration

In the late 1600's, the Dutch physicist Christiaan Huygens observed that the pendulum clocks on one clock shop wall were all synchronized. The swinging pendulums were locked in a common rhythmic mode through sympathetic vibrations carried in the wall.

in common energy patterns. Our common reality is the result of the collective energies. That collective energy varies slightly from one place to another, reflecting the character of local energy sources, but all of us reside in a common sea of subtly shifting energy which is the basis for our reality.

Sound current techniques rely on inner sounds to monitor these energy shifts. Once a practitioner becomes familiar with her sound current's interplay with external energy sources such as landscapes, trees, people and even more exotic forces, she can use it as a barometer, or radar, to track environmental shifts. This information about one's outer, and ultimately inner, world(s) can guide a practitioner into calmer seas.

Exercise
Monitoring Energy with Sound Current

Go for a walk. Monitor shifts in your inner sounds. Listen for changes in volume, tone, pitch, evenness and position. Do this as you:

1. Approach and touch people, animals, trees and other living beings.

2. Go in and out of buildings, such as your home.

3. Enter distinct areas like intersections, a park or your yard.

States Of Energy

How does the energy of the sound current compare with other energies? Obviously, the world is a very diverse place. If everything is energy, how is it that energy takes so many forms? A sound wave is not the same as a light wave. A rock is certainly not the same as light. Our five primary senses each record different types of vibration. Ears vibrate with sounds. Skin resonates with pressure, or touch. Eyes sympathetically vibrate with light energies. How are common threads of energy hidden behind this diversity?

Matter

When a guitar string is vibrating it looks like a smeared-out blur because it is moving so fast. What if you could vibrate a string so fast that it seemed to be everywhere in its vibrating space all at once? It would appear solid. If a stationary source vibrates fast enough, we begin to perceive it as a solid object. This gives us a clue about how energy creates matter.

The formula for creating a small subatomic particle of matter involves smashing two pulses of light together. You can trap the vibrating energy of traveling light waves. It is a bit like holding both ends of a light wave guitar string and plucking it. A kind of *standing wave* results. That wave vibrates so fast that it appears solid.

Standing waves result when trapped waves keep passing through each other at exactly the same place. A standing wave appears to be standing still.

In this way, matter can be created directly from light. Matter is energy totally bounded in our time and space. It vibrates like the guitar string, but so fast that it is solid. Matter is trapped light. The original energy is still there, but we perceive it differently. Its new configuration is more substantial in our reality, existing at a different level of organization. The threads of light energy have been woven in a new way.

Larger objects, like chairs and people, are made of similar small constituent bits of matter. Light energy makes subatomic particles. Subatomic particles make atoms. Atoms make molecules. Molecules make chairs and people. Each new order of energy creates new configurations.

We perceive and interpret each configuration differently. Just as there is a field of energy providing the structural information in the fabric of a small bit of subatomic matter, there is a structural energy field organizing each person. It has a unifying energy principle. Call it a DNA energy pattern or a soul. We are organized, aware conglomerations of energy fields living in a sea of energy.

Cycling Information

Like DNA, all energy is information. When different energies interact, information is communicated. Things organize themselves according to that information. Energy is information that continually rebroadcasts the nature of its existence. Cycling informational energy is somewhat like a hypnotist. The hypnotic message repeats, "I exist, I exist...."

This is how we, as energetic beings, are programmed and program each other about the level of energy we call normal reality. Fortunately, as individuals, we have access to a much broader source of energy. The sound current is infinitely diverse. It mirrors every shifting energy pattern. The sound current offers freedom from mundane local programming, because it gives us a direct link to greater fields of awareness. Unfortunately, this makes the task of fully comprehending its message a daunting one. If one could fully grasp the sound current, it would be as the famous physicist Stephen Hawking said about obtaining the elusive *Theory of Everything*: "...then we would know the mind of God."

Levels of Order

One hope for understanding both physical reality and the sound current lies in a deeper analysis of information theory. As we have seen, there are levels of information. One level of energy organizes light. Another order of energy organizes subatomic particles and so on. Each new level of organization is ordered by a new level of information, or energy.

Remember the weaver's cloth. A pattern of information organizes the threads, but the threads themselves have an internal weave. Each thread is spun from many fibers. Those fibers are in turn ordered by different patterns on the molecular and atomic scales. Finally, at the subatomic level, the cloth's matter is only patterns of trapped light.

If you unraveled the cloth, one level of organizing energy would be gone. You would be left with a pile of threads. If you unravel it at the subatomic level all that would remain is light.

Virtual Reality

Where did the energy go that ordered the cloth and its atoms? In physics, we speak of virtual particle fields. Perhaps the unraveled atoms returned to a virtual state, always there, existing forever, waiting to be again. It may be that mystics hold the sound current in such high esteem because it echoes the virtual state of All That Is, the Vital Essence of Creation.

A Theory Of Everything

However, if we do discover a complete theory...then we would know the mind of God.

— Stephen Hawking
A Brief History Of Time
p. 175

The Way Of Nature

The Tao (Way) that can be told of is not the eternal Tao; The name that can be named is not the eternal name. The Nameless is the origin of Heaven and Earth; The Named is the mother of all things. Therefore let there always be non-being so we may see their subtlety, and let there always be being so we may see their outcome.

— Lao Tzu
Tao-Te Ching
As translated by
— Wing-Tsit Chan
A Source Book In Chinese Philosophy
p. 139

Being told you live in a world which is nothing more than a hierarchy of levels of structural information (i.e., everything is energy) is not much different than a mystic saying everything is illusory, or life is but a dream. Perhaps reality is manifested from a virtual field of energy. As part of that creation, we would automatically be in direct contact with that level of energy. In sound current studies, that connection is the internal sound.

Energy Waves

Physics Perplexed

Given the limitless variety of ways in which matter and energy can arrange themselves, almost all of which would be "random," the fact that the physical world is a coherent collection of mutually tolerant, quasi-stable entities is surely a fact in need of explanation.

— P. C. W. Davies

As Edited By

— Wojciech H. Zurek

Complexity, Entropy, And The Physics Of Information

p. 61

Look at some of the faces of energy in nature. Studying different states of energy in familiar objects can reconnect our rational and intuitive conceptions of reality.

One of the most common states of energy is the traveling wave. The world around us contains many obvious examples of traveling energy waves. Drop a rock onto the surface of a pond. Circling waves spread out in ever-widening rings. Stand by the ocean. Long waves roll in and dissipate on the shore with a resounding roar.

Waves on a String

One easy way to see how energy waves travel is by observing an energy pulse on a string. Take a long string. Hold it by one end, and give it a flip. The motion of your hand sends an energy wave down the string. You have created a traveling wave of mechanical energy. The energy wave on the string was created by the mechanical energy of your flipping hand. That energy then traveled away from its source, your hand, down the string.

Light Waves

Light also travels in waves. The difference is that light waves involve electricity and magnetism, which require no known physical medium to travel: no strings attached.

To create a light wave you "flip" an electric charge. The resulting electromagnetic wave then travels through space. However, flipping a charged particle and creating a light wave visible to the human eye is a little tricky. You have to flip it

$$1,000,000,000,000,000$$

times per second. That is a frequency within the visible light spectrum. Even for the highly dexterous this would be challenging, to say the least.

Electrons

However, nature possesses sufficient dexterity. It makes light by vibrating electrically charged subatomic particles called electrons. When an electron inside an atom accumulates too much energy and vibrates too fast, it becomes unstable. It flips the extra energy away as a traveling pulse of light. This goes on every time you turn on a light switch. The electricity heats up the filament in the light bulb. Then the electrons get frantic and throw out the extra energy as light.

People who hear the sound current are sometimes a bit like an excited electron, over energized in some way. They are approaching a state change. Similar to the excited electron, they can become a little frantic. Excess energy is registered as feedback in the shifting levels, or tones, of their sound current.

Energy Beings

Humans are amazing creatures. Our bodies give off infrared heat. Our spines emanate microwaves. Our nervous systems and brains are such elaborate electrical systems that they are barely understood. Who knows what kinds of energies they might produce?

We vibrate in innumerable ways. Our energy mingles with the Cosmos in unfathomable patterns. We receive and broadcast vast sums of information. At the edge of normal conscious perception there is a palpable energy called the sound current.

New Realities

The most difficult problem...concerning the use of the language arises in quantum theory. Here we have at first no simple guide for correlating the mathematical symbols with concepts of ordinary language; and the only thing we know from the start is the fact that our common concepts cannot be applied to the structure of the atoms.

— W. Heisenberg
As recorded by
— Fritjof Capra
The Tao Of Physics
p. 45

The Spectrum Of Reality

Bound energy radiates information about its presence. Light waves travel through space, but light trapped as matter emits a gravity field. Though we all know how gravity behaves, science does not know how to produce it. Gravity may be our most common experience of energy, but it is a great mystery to science. If the true nature of this most common form of energy has yet to be rationally explained, what other energy structures lie behind reality which have yet to be discovered by science?

Everything creates energy fields. Biological organisms have extremely complex fields. Scientists can even detect all sorts of energy fields around human beings. But what kinds of energy fields organize the Cosmos? The closest science has come to detecting an omnipresent energy field, which contains all the structural information required to make the Cosmos, is the universal background radiation discussed in Chapter One. Physical science is lagging behind mysticism in this area.

Our seen and unseen environments are a cacophony of natural and human-made information. In the spectrum of vibrating electromagnetic energy our eyes perceive only a tiny band called visible light. Infrared light is a lower vibratory state that we feel as heat. The energies that we can perceive with our bodies represent only a tiny fraction of those discovered by science.

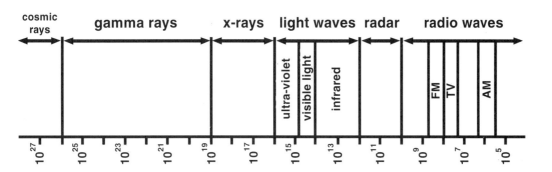

Wave Frequencies

The Electromagnetic Spectrum

This spectrum is the gambit of traveling energies that have both electrical and magnetic waves. The two wave components create and sustain each other. The only difference between our "visible" colors and "invisible" radio waves is the frequency of the waves. The frequency superscript numbers indicate how many zeros come after each 10. For example, the frequency of visible red light is about a ten with fourteen zeros after it in vibrations per second.

Sound Current Energy

All aspects of physical reality can be analyzed through the study of energy. Energy, that vital force which lies behind everything, can come forward into grosser aspects of physical manifestation to form matter. Everything around us is energy in some form. Light is a traveling wave of electromagnetic energy. Matter is trapped light energy. Science continues to probe deeper into the mysteries of our universe. Along the way, new expressions of energy are constantly being discovered.

The Future

The rational understanding of energy was an amazing conceptual leap for modern humanity. Intuitive notions of what lies behind acts of nature can now be comprehended by the rational mind. Science has demonstrated that reality is far more elaborate than the world we commonly experience. It is poised to confirm and validate experiences which were previously solely in the domain of mystics.

The universal background radiation is the echo of the physical universe's creation. Perhaps the sound current is the background energy field in a larger Cosmos, a universe of universes, in which our physical reality is but one possible interpretation of existence.

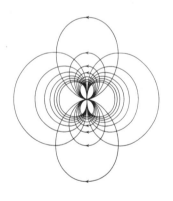

Energy fields radiate outward or curve back in on themselves, like the bar magnet above. Some fields radiate out and yet do not seem to deplete the energy of their sources, unlike the guitar string. All matter produces gravitational fields, but matter does not seem to lose energy in the process.

All *energy fields* connect with all other energy fields, either by a direct exchange of information, or by indirectly bleeding through into each other's fields. The Cosmos is a sea of energy. Information is exchanged between everything and everything else. We sense and exchange energy with the totality of our environment. Some of the mechanisms of those exchanges are known to science, others are not. Just because science has yet to prove the sound current does not mean it is not there.

Scientists tend to fall into two groups. One group believes almost everything has been figured out, and has proclaimed so throughout science's history. The other is awed by the mystery of it all and expects new breakthroughs every day. I definitely fall into the second group. I believe the bigger picture is always just coming into view. The horizon is ever widening. We can assume there are energy spectrums science does not yet know about. As soon as science seriously looks for more esoteric forms of energy, it will find them. Among them will be the sound current.

Someday we will have a device capable of picking up the sound current the way our televisions confirm the existence of the electromagnetic broadcast waves. That day has not yet arrived. When it comes, I think we will find that the sound current is our key to the Cosmos.

To see a world in a grain of sand
And a heaven in a wild flower,
Hold infinity in the palm of
your hand
And eternity in an hour.

— William Blake
Auguries of Innocence

CHAPTER SIX

Perception

The Science and Art of Personal Reality

How do we perceive the sound current? The mysteries of the sound current spring from the very foundations of reality. To understand the sound current, we must understand the act of perception. Most people take the "world" for granted. But we have revealed each reality to be a complex energyscape. The worlds we live in are mental constructs gleaned from a sea of information through acts of perception.

We have looked at the outer energy environment. Now we must peer into the inner world of personal perception. This is the other half of the reality equation. How do we, en masse and as individuals, convert raw information into the stuff of our lives? And where does the sound current fit in?

The Barrier Of Perception

"Now the only thing left for you to do before the explanation of the mastery of awareness is complete," he went on, *"is to break the barrier of perception by yourself.... Not to do this will turn everything you've done with me into merely talk...."*

— Carlos Castaneda
The Fire From Within
p. 256

Beings Of Perception

We are creatures of perception. When people speak of subjective reality, they are normally referring to individual systems of interpretation. Each of us makes a personal interpretation of the information we receive about the outside world. A snake may be fascinating to one person and terrifying to another. There may be biases of culture or personal experience. The familiar smells of home, which give rise to feelings of security to the returning traveler, might be offensive to his foreign guests.

Subjective Reality

In discussions about the subjective nature of reality, it is generally assumed that all parties are receiving the same outside stimuli. The environment is expected to be a dependable constant. Differing opinions about the character of the outside world are attributed to different systems of interpretation or sensory capabilities. One person's view could vary because of colorblindness, for example. Few suspect that the relationship between environment and personal reality is not only tremendously complicated, but totally interactive as well. Between the outer and inner realities lies the act of perception.

Personal Reality

There is no effect in the exterior world that does not spring from an inner source. There is no motion that does not first occur within the mind.

— Jane Roberts
The Nature Of Personal Reality
p. 3

Internal Meets External

In physics, the concepts of action and reaction express a balancing of physical energies. Spiritual teachings, and some physicists, go a step further, suggesting a connection between thought and reality. Internal and external realities are closely linked. Both physics and metaphysics deal with objective reality as an external energy statement, the outer sea of energy. Common experience leads us to believe that objective reality is independent of our existence, and that the outer world is somehow immutable and exists separately from all observers. Neither physicists nor mystics support this idea.

Observer and Observed

Modern physics asserts that the observed is not independent of the observer. Each observation affects the object being observed. One must rely on the transfer of energy to receive information about an object. The very act of acquiring that information affects the balance of energy in the system being observed. One cannot "touch" a system to observe it without affecting it. To observe is to participate. In fact, to exist is to participate.

Existence

Modern physics and ancient mysticism both tell us that a pure objective outer reality, a reality that exists independently of any observer, does not exist. But we certainly exist. As Descartes stated, "I think, therefore I am." The fact that we exist means we have an impact on the system we are observing.

We each affect reality, both personally and en masse. Each individual is a separate observer. Each individual affects what he or she is observing, including the other observers. We all affect each other in an infinitely complex web of information exchange. In the midst of this infinitely complex energy web, there is no objective universe that we can determine from our vantage point inside the web. There is no normal reality.

The Narrow Band of Reality

We are masters of specialized perception. Just as our physical eyes operate in a very narrow band of the spectrum of electromagnetic radiation, our conscious awareness operates in a narrow band called normal reality. Even on this mundane level, our five physical senses take in far more information than we can consciously comprehend.

This can be demonstrated with hypnosis. Under hypnosis, a witness may remember a particular incident and, for example, recall the number on a passing license plate. A great deal of information is received and stored in subconscious memory, to which the conscious mind is not normally privy.

Pertinent Information

Our overall awareness processes a sum of information that is unmanageable to the conscious awareness. Look at the autistic savant. He may be able to tell you what the weather

Infinite Worlds

Heisenberg's uncertainty principle is a concept that reflects the inability to predict the future based on the past or based on the present…. It is the cornerstone of quantum physics and provides an understanding of why the world is made of events that cannot be related entirely in terms of cause and effect.

— Fred Alan Wolf

Parallel Universes: The Search for Other Worlds

p. 43

report was every day for the past ten years, but the ability to function socially is overwhelmed by the plethora of data available to his conscious mind, a deluge of information normally screened out by the so-called "healthy" mind. The normal mind skims the mass of available data and passes on only the bits of information it considers pertinent.

What is pertinent? Our genetic heritage makes survival and procreation paramount. Our social programming dictates the importance of interpersonal interactions. All this we call normal living.

It is within the area of social programming that the average person strives to better himself. We seek to improve our systems of interpretation, continually upgrading the meaning we prescribe to the information we receive about the surrounding world. This is the socially mandated method of self-improvement. However, it is not the mystic's way.

Other Choices

There is another area of human development with potentially far greater consequences. We are beings of energy. All of reality is an energy construct. We, as perceivers, are detectors, interpreters and stalkers of energy. The light reaching your eye is a wave of vibrating energy, but more than that, every observable phenomenon is energy. Light is traveling energy. Matter consists of stationary fields of energy. Matter is created from light. This is not philosophy, this is physics.

In a Cosmos of energy, questions regarding the nature of reality become questions of energy perception or interaction. If

---

Remembering Non-ordinary Reality

Castaneda: *I could not recall the feeling that had flooded me just moments ago....*

don Juan: *"You're going the wrong way," don Juan said. "You're trying to remember thoughts in the way you normally do, but this is a different situation....You have to recall them by 'intending' them back."*

— Carlos Castaneda

The Power Of Silence: Further Lessons of don Juan

p. 84

---

our minds skim out all but the pertinent data for our conscious perusal, what is the greater picture?

In our normal, selective mode of perception we essentially experience only those stimuli bearing directly on our physical and social survival. The rich fabric of our larger existence is hidden from us in our quest to maintain the integrity of the one thread we call normal physical reality. Historically, we have expended our personal energy protecting our investment in the reality held by the mass consciousness. Yet we have access to a much larger energy spectrum. The hum of the sound current is a signpost pointing the way to these greater possibilities.

As creatures of perception, we have the ability to select our mode of perceiving. In order to perceive, we tune into specific energy bands. This is similar to aligning a television antenna with a particular broadcasting station. Normally, we align with the energy fields the mass consciousness is fixated on. The bulk of humanity is tuned to a specific energy channel. Within that narrow band of energy we skim off the pertinent data, organize it through our learned system of interpretation, and assemble our view of reality.

Systems of Interpretation

Systems of interpretation are learned and maintained by social conditioning, but the combined energetic pressure of the masses fixes the specific energy fields used to assemble normal reality. This mass fixation is generally overwhelming.

Just as with the earth, where so much magnetic material is aligned north and south that a magnetized compass needle automatically tries to achieve the same alignment, so it is with people. We naturally align to the prevailing forces.

Observation Affects Reality

"Experiments have revealed that when you break apart small aspects of energy, what we call elementary particles, and try to observe how they operate, the act of observation itself alters the results - as if these elementary particles are influenced by what the experimenter expects."

— James Redfield

The Celestine Prophecy: An Adventure

p. 42

**Intent:
Thought Energy**

"In other words, the basic stuff of the universe, at its core, is looking like a kind of pure energy that is malleable to human intention and expectation in a way that defies our old mechanistic model of the universe - as though our expectation itself causes our energy to flow out into the world and affect other energy systems."

— James Redfield

*The Celestine Prophecy:
An Adventure*

p. 42

Systems of Reality

There are, however, other energetic options. Truly amazing results are possible through shifting to frequencies beyond normal perception. One may gain far greater clarity about the world we live in, or shift awareness to entirely different systems. The sound current is the key.

The sound current is an audible readout of your energy state. When your tone shifts, your perception of energy shifts. Most valid descriptions of altered states and spiritual journeys describe audible shifts in the sound current. Those who make such shifts in consciousness without noticing sound changes are so completely immersed in the flow of the sound current that they cannot detect ambient differences. They have no reference point because of their total immersion in the energy stream.

Interpreting Reality

Everything is made up of energy. Energy vibrates. Everything in the Cosmos vibrates. Every aspect of reality is continually broadcasting information about the nature of its existence. On the broadest scale, this information reaches us through the sound current. In our immediate physical environments, simpler orders of information reach us through our five ordinary senses.

Some of this simpler information can pass through the air as sound waves. When those sound waves reach our ears, the vibrations are converted into electrical energy. These electrical signals then pass through auditory nerves into our brains. There the information is given personal meaning.

We use that processed sensory input to construct an image of our environment. Each of us recreates the outer world in our own mind. The resulting worldview is thus highly personal. It is filled with information relative to us as individuals. Only those objects that the individual psyche considers most meaningful populate each internal landscape.

So, the act of perception involves more than simply receiving energy from the outside world. An internal system of interpretation is applied to the data. That system of interpretation mirrors everything we are as social creatures, biological entities and energetic beings. It reflects our biological and social heritage.

This heritage represents a kind of programming. A great deal of our personal makeup has been predetermined. We are programmed to behave in certain ways. Some behaviors can be ascribed to genetic predilections carried in our *DNA*. This programming represents our biological evolution. It speaks for everything we are as human animals. Actually, "speaks," as we shall see, may not be the appropriate word. Our basic instinctive functions evolved before the power of speech.

DNA, or deoxyribonucleic acid, is a molecular double helix inside the chromosomes of each living cell's nuclei which transmits hereditary patterns.

The Biology Of Perception

Our biology dictates much of how we view ourselves in the physical world. So let us take a brief look into the biology of our perception. The energy structure we call the brain is a natural place to conduct our search for genetic components of personal perception.

Spiritual Heritage

The communicator of biological heredity was a great mystery until the discovery of DNA. The sound current is the communicator of our spiritual heritage, but it has yet to be detected by science.

The Caduceus, or staff, of the ancient Egyptian healer-priest Tehuty is now the symbol of the medical profession. It represents two energy channels in the human body. The reptilian energy entwines the spine with a DNA like double helix. The heads of the snakes are just above the ears running up to the crown of the head, the line where sound is normally perceived.

Genetic Programming

All life seeks energy and its vitality. Living beings are attracted to beneficial energy connections. For all forms of life, this is an issue of survival. We require energy to survive. We avoid connections that prove detrimental. Our bodies assist us with their innate intelligence, communicating with us through conditioned responses. We seek pleasure and avoid pain. Pleasure and pain are the language of our bodies. Through these sensations, our bodies communicate their needs and help us manage our connections in the external world.

We have evolved in a predatory environment. Our genetic programming reflects our long heritage of seeking survival. An aspect of that survival is reproduction. Another part is acquiring energy from other life forms to sustain our own. Everything is food for something else. We have evolved as predator and prey, with eons of primitive survival representing the vast majority of our history. Yet the history of civilized Homo sapiens is a relatively small time period in the overall scheme. Our languages, arts and sciences are but recent advents.

Three Brains

The way we have evolved has great bearing on how we receive and process information from the world around us. We process information at several levels. Some of these levels are conscious while others are subconscious. This hierarchy is dramatically illustrated in the structure of our brains. Our brain really consists of three brains. Each has developed separately to interpret more and more complex levels of thought energy. They are:

1. The ancient reptilian brain.
2. The limbic brain.
3. The more recent neocortex.

Reptilian Brain

The reptilian brain is similar to that of the dinosaurs. It controls body functions, such as movement and tissue regeneration. It is an instinctive brain of patterned responses. Without the more evolved ability to evaluate decisions, habitually repeating successful behavior patterns is critical to the survival of the primitive reptilian brain. This is the territorial dragon within us that can smell fear and possesses ancient knowledge. The dragon thinks in pictures; speech is a higher function. Our reptilian nature is ritualistic, willful and direct.

Limbic Brain

The warm-blooded mammals that inherited the earth following the demise of the dinosaurs grew larger brains. The limbic brain processes a more complex level of mental alternatives called emotions. Emotions are not mere yes/no informational responses. These are sophisticated story pictures. Life's subtle hues lie in the limbic brain, alongside our fears and superstitions. The limbic brain is a kind of amplifier for the reptilian brain. The reptilian brain's digital processes are magnified until they become an analog balancing act, the source of our dramatic natures.

Neocortex

One hundred thousand years ago, Homo sapiens' brain inexplicably doubled in size. The neocortex evolved with the capacity for abstract thought and self-reflection. The right and left hemispheres provide mathematics and speech; the mysterious frontal lobe perhaps provides forethought. With the neocortex we can ponder the colorful data of the limbic brain and the instincts of the reptilian brain. It gives us the ability to assess our position in the Cosmos.

Taming The Dragon

This snake-brain is charmed when it catches the Word. It is attracted by the sweet Sound of the Word, hearing which it is rendered motionless and the soul is released from bondage.

— Kirpal Singh

As compiled by

— Ruth Seader

The Teachings Of Kirpal Singh Volume II

p. 101

Reptilian Nature

And thus in fire and in darkness was the Dragon born. Her nature bears everlasting testimony to that uneasy birth, and ever after, no other creature has possessed the same measure of strength and cunning.

— Michael Green

De Historia Et Veritate Unicornis: On the History and Truth of the Unicorn

p. 23

The Conscious Mind

Each of our sub-brains manages information from the outside world. Just as different levels of structure in the physical world are determined by orders of energy, each sub-brain processes different types of thought energy. Collectively, they allow us to survive and prosper by presenting a coherent picture of the energy around us. The sensory data is processed, filtered and compiled for conscious review. Our conscious minds only acknowledge a fraction of the initial information. We do not perceive outside energy directly. What we call the world is a highly interpreted mental construct, a model we take to be reality. We interact with our model rather than directly with the energy at large.

The Character of Our Human Hardware

Much of the character of our perception is biologically mandated. The structure of our brains is analogous to the architecture of a computer. The very design of the neuro-pathways biases the outcome of the processed information. Each component of our brains influences our thought process, together creating a synergistic organ. Our worldview is a collaboration, a symphony of information systems. Each sub-brain acts independently yet in concert.

When you touch something hot, your hand acts to remove itself from danger before your higher brain functions are even involved. By the time you realize what is burning you, your hand has long since removed itself from danger. Your instinctive brain takes care of immediate survival issues. Information about how you feel about those events comes from your emotional brain. Your neocortex allows you to learn from the situation and decide how to deal with it.

A Shaman's Journey

As I started upward into the darkness, faint lines of light appeared. They grew sharper and more intricate, and burst into brilliant colors. Sound came from far away, a sound like a waterfall, which grew stronger until it filled my ears.

— Michael Harner

The Way Of The Shaman

p. 2

We represent a complex amalgam of thought patterns. On one level, things that are not pertinent to fighting, feeding, fleeing or reproduction receive less attention. At another level, we have evolved the capacity to create art and music, and yet, those very expressions reflect the primitive energy connections which bind us to the outer world.

Screening Reality

Each sub-brain and level of data transfer has the capacity to screen out data. Incoming information therefore passes through many screens. Your instinctual, emotional and rational brains all filter information. What proceeds to your conscious mind is the cream of the processed information, high priority action items. What does not get through is everything that does not stand out from the background. The sound current is normally in the background. In fact, it is the background.

Receiving the Sound Current

Most people do not consciously perceive the sound current. It is filtered out on a subconscious level. As an example of how this happens, listen to a spiral seashell. The *white noise* it produces is an amplification of the sound of moving air. A similar noise occurs in your own ears. It is always there, but you do not hear it. The reason you are not aware of its presence is that your brain does not consider it critical to your physical well-being, since it does not require conscious attention or action. The information is regarded as non-threatening, monotonous, background noise. It is considered superfluous and is therefore disregarded. It never reaches you on a conscious level.

But if a strong wind picks up, then that is a survival issue. Your brain is interested in threatening weather conditions. Suddenly, you hear the sound of moving air very well, because it

The Feel Of Energy

Energy is Eternal Delight.
— William Blake

White noise is a completely random mix over a wide range of frequencies. The sounds of ocean surf are sometimes referred to as white noise.

is above normal background limits. But when our systems are running within normal tolerances, background information is not reported to the conscious mind. People talking in the background, strangers walking by, and the general hubbub of life do not affect us. We are barely aware of these things unless something attracts our attention to them. For example, if someone points out a stranger to you, you take note of that person's appearance and mannerisms. You consciously focus on the stranger.

So it is with the sound current. It is always there, in the background, but we do not generally notice. When we are quiet and background noises seem amplified, or something happens to elevate the power level of the sound current, then it pops out from the general milieu to be consciously perceived as ringing, buzzing, humming, roaring or any number of manifestations.

The Psychology Of Perception

At the apex of our biology rests personal psychology: who we are as individuals. If our brains are the hardware of our mental computers, social programming is the software. We have been trained to acknowledge sensory input in certain ways. Any data outside those parameters is considered superfluous by the mind.

The way we maintain personal and consensual reality is through a process of selective data skimming. This occurs at a subconscious level, but it can be consciously programmed. We are socially programmed by outside influences, but it is a conscious choice to internalize those messages.

Programming from Within

Earlier I related a story from my childhood about the sound current involving my mother. In that experience, I had been perfectly calm and quite curious about the sound current before witnessing my mother's negative reaction. That story is an example of an overt way to program a child not to perceive information which does not relate to the common mass reality.

In that situation, I allowed my fear of my mother's reaction to override my natural curiosity. Rather than continuing to investigate the sound current, I chose to suppress the experience. My mother provided the social programming, but I consciously internalized the information. It descended into the subconscious lair of my protector dragon (i.e., my reptilian brain), because my conscious awareness indicated that it could not resolve the conflict. What cannot be dealt with on a conscious level submerges into the subconscious. For me, the result was that I lost touch with the sound current for many years. I retreated back into the box of normal reality.

The Spirituality Of Perception

Human nature is an elaborate combination of forces. At the roots of our cognitive processes, we skim information and reinterpret our world. The prejudices of childhood, and the cultural biases acquired through the experiences of our lives, are only some of the factors that dictate the meaning and degrees of importance we ascribe to the objects and circumstances around us. Some of these conjectures we make at a conscious level, but most are made subconsciously. All are unique and completely individual.

Reprogramming The Subconscious

If our primitive brain, our unconscious mind, expresses itself through symbols during our dreams, can we not use our neocortex to string symbols together to communicate with it? If we can consciously communicate with our primitive brains...can we not reprogram them?

— Alberto Villoldo
The Four Winds: A Shaman's Odyssey into the Amazon
p. 129

Individuality

Somehow the individual is greater than the sum of his or her parts. Biology and social programming cannot completely account for what makes each of us a unique human being. This is true because we possess independent volition, free will. We can pattern our destiny through conscious intent. Our intent then determines the nature of our connection with the energy around us.

Totality of Being

Our entire connection with the Cosmos is revealed in the sound current. In our vast hierarchy of information processing stages, the sound current is the one constant. Through it we link with what mystics have called the "Totality of the Absolute."

As human creatures, we flatten our innate multidimensional knowing into a three-dimensional world. As spiritual beings, we have the opportunity to bring greater knowing into direct conscious awareness. The sound current offers that opportunity. It is the key that allows us to enter into our highest nature.

Energy, Emotion And Matter

Emotion is energy in motion. When you move your energy, you create effect. If you move enough energy, you create matter. Matter is energy conglomerated.... It is the alchemy of the universe. It is the secret of life.

— Neale Donald Walsch
Conversations With God: Book I
p. 54

PERCEPTION

You listen for sounds such as a roar of the Ocean, or a bell ringing, or thunder, or bees buzzing. In time one of these sounds will come. Some perhaps hear one sound first, then another; others may hear a different sound first. When this sound comes, put your whole attention on it, and in doing this you become "baptized."

— Dr. Quantz Crawford
Methods Of Psychic Development
p. 30

CHAPTER SEVEN

Perceiving The Sound Current

The Nature of the Audible Life Stream

The sound current is not a malady. Becoming aware of it means that you are in contact with extraordinary energy. You are widening, or changing, your band of perception. You are adjusting your personal energy to match external conditions.

You experience subtle energy shifts all the time. Normally this is accommodated subconsciously, much as body temperature is regulated. When your connection with the larger energy picture alters dramatically, you become consciously aware of the energy flux. This energy flux is most easily perceived as a shift in the sound current.

It is like floating in a rowboat down a gentle river. Normally you watch the events on the passing shores, oblivious to the placid water. But the waters are not always the same. Sometimes your boat rushes along on swifter currents. You notice the water on those days. Occasionally there are wide calm places, with still waters barely moving. In those peaceful times you might contemplate life slowly unfolding on the shore. Other days, there are little eddies, some days quietly turning whirlpools. You listen to the gurgling, playful flow. Once in a while you run through rapids. On those exhilarating days, all your attention is riveted on the churning waters. You hear every sound of its rushing energy. Shooting through tumultuous currents toward new horizons is a life altering experience. Knowing the nature of the waters is the key to success.

The scenes unfolding along the banks of this imaginary waterway are the stories of our lives. The shoreline is the illusory

Sound Meditation

In the course of active meditation, there are many phenomena which you will encounter. One of these is the 'Nada,' or sound current. The Nada is a vibrational current, a ripple of sound, if you will, which courses through absolutely everything.

— Christopher S. Kilham

Inner Power: Secrets from Tibet and the Orient

p. 114

construct, where we meet up with fellow travelers who follow other byways. The waters beneath us are the energies of creation, the ebb and flow of the Cosmos. The boat each of us rides on is the platform of inner Self from which we experience the Cosmos. We are free to ride into infinity. We are creatures of choice only if we choose to be. We can flounder and go where fate takes us, or learn the ways of the waters and navigate towards a destiny of our choosing.

Navigating The Sound Current

The sound current is our connecting link with the energy flow of the Cosmos. The sounds we perceive, as our conscious awareness approaches it, are the first palpable signs of its presence.

Hearing the Sound Current

The sound current is not a normal sound. Hearing the sound current is a matter of intent. You must go within and intend to hear it. Doing so does not diminish normal hearing. These inner sounds can be mentally distracting if one struggles against the sound current, but they do not actually interfere with ordinary hearing. Perception of normal outside sounds occurs on a different perceptual track. This is one way to separate the act of "hearing the sound current" from cases of degenerative dysfunctions.

Sound Current Logos

Each living creature is the channel for a current of life-force which proceeds from the Logos, the Creator of this universe.

— Dion Fortune

Psychic Self-Defense

p. 122

Calling the sound current a sound, and referring to the process of perceiving it as "hearing," is equivalent to using the term "seeing" to describe a daydream. The process "feels" like hearing, just as daydreaming, or recalling a scene from memory, "feels" like seeing. We speak of the mind's eye. We may say that we first perceive the sound current with the mind's ear. Our minds interpret the information as sound, but there is no sound, at least not in the normal sense.

118

Seeing the Sound Current

This may come as a bizarre revelation to some, but you can also see the sound current. The name "sound current" and other traditional names used to describe our topic refer to its characteristic sounds. But the sound current is pure energy. It may be processed in the brain as auditory or visual information. Visual processing just requires more familiarity, or intuitive clarity.

Exercise
Gaining Insight

The way to achieve greater clarity is to intend it and listen. Let go of the idea that you will hear better by straining harder with your ears. Reach into the sound with your awareness. Connect to the sound current with your sense of being. Use your feelings to guide you. As you do so, lightly observe the images arising in your mind. After you have focused your thoughts on your intention to gather clear information, relax and be open. Listen to what comes.

Visions

Yoda: *Through the Force, things you will see, other places, the future, the past, old friends long gone.*

— George Lucas
The Empire Strikes Back

The trouble is, we focus on familiar patterns as we reach for a new way of paying attention. It is like tuning your radio to a new station. You have to let go of the old station. You must enter into a new energy configuration. Your inner Self already knows how.

**Many Mansions,
Many Worlds**

*I was never sure what sort
of energies I would
encounter in these realms.
Each "world" had its own
rules and operating
instructions. Some of the
worlds were joyful and
light, while others were
absolutely terrifying.*

— Dr. Susan Gregg

*Dance Of Power:
A Shamanic Journey*

p. 10

Thought Train

New students often tell me, "I saw something, but I thought it was just my imagination." That is what our minds tell us at first. It takes time to separate incoming information from your own internal thought processes and trust in these new perceptions. To determine the origin of a thought, analyze its development. Your thoughts normally follow a natural progression. If a fully developed thought image springs into your mind from nowhere, it probably originated from an outside source.

Imperfect Outside Information

Not all outside information comes directly from the sound current. You continually receive thought patterns from others. Telepathy is not widely acknowledged, so we do not monitor the sources of our thoughts. We assume that anything arising in our minds is the result of our own thoughts. Often, this is not the case. Just because it is in your head does not mean you put it there.

Thought waves and other energies flowing through us are normally processed subconsciously. Becoming telepathic, clairvoyant or communing with the sound current is not a matter of acquiring a new sense. It involves consciously acknowledging the information already available to you. This may be a new listening skill, but the reception is already happening. Focusing on the information in the sound current is the key to learning to shift your perception.

It is like buying a new automobile. Suddenly, you notice the make of your new car everywhere you go. When your awareness takes in something new, you are keyed into it. You find it everywhere. It is the same when you truly discover the sound current and step beyond the ordinary.

Use Discretion

Always use your best judgment. Receiving information internally does not guarantee its value. The clearer your connection with the sound current, the better the information. Be discerning. Follow you heart. Keep your thoughts and intentions positive.

The Force Is With You

People struggle to not perceive what they consider impossible. People who hear the sound current often are not convinced that they are perceiving something "real." It is presumed that because no apparent outside source exists, then it must be a defect associated with the hearing process.

The idea of perceiving an omnipresent energy field is not usually the first thing that enters people's minds. Rather they try to avoid contact with the sound current, as they do with all events outside their socially mandated reality. In spite of this, it is impressive, in our culture of spiritual denial, how many people instinctively know there is deep meaning in those itinerant sounds.

Most of us still have to get past our social programming. Once students of sound current become aware of the possibilities of visions and insights, they begin to perceive a wider spectrum of reality that includes mystic events.

The Source Of The Sound Current

In the right conditions almost everyone will hear the sound current. It is always there. The sound current is a real phenomenon. But the question remains, "Where is its source?"

The Force Of Creation

Obi-Wan: *Remember, the Force will be with you always.*

— George Lucas
Star Wars

It [OM or sound current]
*is unperceived by the
sensory organs,
incomprehensible by the
material mind, unthinkable
by thought, indescribable by
tongue and pen, unrelated
to any object, and it is
uninferrable. It is the
essential nature of the
conscious and unconscious
universe. It is the nucleus of
the Self....you must realize
it for your liberation.*

— Rammurti S. Mishra,
M.D.

*Fundamentals Of Yoga:
A Handbook of Theory
and Application*

p. 137

Inner and Outer

We resonate with the sound current through sympathetic vibrations. We receive it and broadcast it. We are recipient and source, radio and broadcasting station.

This is the nature of the sound current. "All That Is" creates it. Each component of the Cosmos receives the sound current, imbues the energy according to its own nature, and transmits a unique energetic contribution back to the Cosmos.

The sound current is the energy signature of the Cosmos. Since all that exists is energy, in a sense, the sound current is the Cosmos. The sound current creates the Cosmos and is created by it. It is the primal tone which created the first resonance. It sets everything in motion, both physical and nonphysical. Yet, the source of the sound current is All That Is.

Specific Sounds

Our ears detect motion, or energy waves, in the air. The sound current is motion, but not motion in the normal physical world. Corroborating its existence can be difficult. Perception of the sound current is individualized but not random. The cacophony of energetic events in our immediate environments strongly affects our link with the Cosmos. Sudden changes in tonal quality and volume are often noticed by an entire group of intuitive individuals.

Any event could trigger an increase in the sound current. You might connect energetically with an approaching person, or pass through an energetically significant area. Our energy systems are always seeking equilibrium with the surroundings. External energies, which we do not quickly and smoothly balance with, can cause a dramatic response in our own energy. Listening to the sound current is a method of monitoring your energy equilibrium. If it jumps in volume, or frequency, you are making an energy connection that is not routine.

Emotional thoughts can affect your sound current. A shift in your energy may cause a response in someone else's. Your wonderful thought may create a higher, finer tone in your companions.

When I am with other meditators, I frequently mention sudden changes in my perception of the sound current. Almost without fail, others have also noticed a change. However, the specifics are apt to receive less confirmation. One person may say the sound became louder while another may have noticed the sudden appearance of new tones.

On hikes, I like to ask people about their sounds as they pass between two trees. Trees often set up very noticeable connections with each other. A person's sound usually jumps when walking between them.

Unintentional Connections

It is when there is a strong power surge that the increased flow is unavoidable, such as the ones caused by some narcotics, or a stressful power demand, such as those resulting from suffering a traumatic shock. Health, or internal emotional issues, affect our tones. Our energy responds to internal and external environments. In turn, each affects the other. Everything is a spiritual event and everything has a physical component. When it comes to the sound current, you cannot separate your daily life from your spiritual life.

Moving Into Energy Fields

The Being of Light was vibrating. As we moved upward, that vibration increased, and the sound emanating from the Being became louder and higher-pitched.

— Dannion Brinkley
Saved By The Light
p. 193

Perceiving the Sound Current En Masse

Our modern lives and culture are riddled with sensory overload. This is why so many are sharing in an experience which was previously almost exclusively in the domain of mystics. Mystics found the phenomenon of the sound current by studying how to shift states of awareness. Modern society is finding it by living in intense energy environments. The mystic's contact with the sound current was induced on a personal level. The situation today is being induced on a mass social scale, most would say by accident. Regardless of the cause, millions of people have been put in direct contact with an energetic phenomenon that can have profound results.

The Nature Of The Sound Current

The sound current represents a communion between each of us as individuals and the forces of creation at large. I previously spoke of the universal background radiation discovered by cosmologists. The sound current is the energy field that contains all other fields in the Cosmos. Perhaps we could call it the carrier wave upon which all other information resides. It is the energy field in which all other energy travels. If energy can be seen as waves on a pond, then the sound current could be likened to the pond itself. Our perceptions of the sound current are glimpses into the Cosmic Field of Creation.

Each of us lives in a subjective world comprised of independently constructed symbols of reality, co-created in conjunction with everyone and everything. En masse we are now entering into a direct relationship with the Source of that creative energy. Our planet is on the threshold of a new awakening.

The United Nations declared just before the new millennium that the world population had officially passed six billion.

The Harmonic Convergence and other names have been coined in connection with the increasing energy pressures which are shifting human consciousness. The shifts seem to be climbing exponentially. Many have noticed increasingly dramatic differences since the mid-1980s.

It had a music that was beyond
any music made by man and
which drew the soul towards
Itself.

— Kirpal Singh

As compiled by
— Ruth Seader
The Teachings Of Kirpal Singh
Volume II
p. 91

CHAPTER EIGHT

Secret Knowledge

Hiding the Truth

Though its study has ancient roots, giving any kind of historic account of the sound current is a difficult task. Information on the sound current, or those who have studied it, is shrouded in myth and mystery.

It is a little like tracking the mythical unicorn. Only occasionally does one catch faint glimpses of the elusive beast, but signs of its presence are everywhere. So it is with the sound current. Specific information is rare in the spiritual literature, but allusions to the sound current abound. The history of the sound current is subtly woven into the history of the world's mystic traditions.

The faintest tracks of our elusive quarry can be found in such magic places as traditional sacred music and creation stories. Ancient spiritual texts make direct references to sound as power or awareness. Exploring myths pertaining to the creative and destructive power of the spoken word is also most illuminating. There we see direct references to the omnipresent sound current.

Schools dedicated to the study of the sound current have also produced a wealth of knowledge. In preparation for our journey into the mystic roots of the sound current, let us first examine the question of why information on the sound current is so well hidden.

Searching For Enlightenment

Along the riverbank under the trees, I discover footprints! Even under the fragrant grass I see his prints.... These traces no more can be hidden than one's nose, looking heavenward.

— Kakuan

A Chinese Zen master in the twelfth century.

As compiled by

— Paul Reps

Zen Flesh, Zen Bones: A Collection Of Zen And Pre-Zen Writings

p. 138

Hidden Wisdom

Shamanic Wisdom Revealed

In recent years, shamans from all over the world have come forward with traditionally secret native healing and soul journeying practices. They maintain that they wish to help modern civilization find balance with nature.

Nada is a Sanskrit term meaning "sound."

...nad(a)-manifestation in sound of the highest psychic energy (prana) which may be heard in one form within the body....

— Rammurti S. Mishra, M.D.

Fundamentals of Yoga: A Handbook of Theory and Application

p. 187

If the sound current is so ubiquitous, why have I never heard of it? The first and most obvious reason we have already touched upon. People are reluctant to discuss private perceptions which they do not consider part of everyone else's normal reality. The sound current is one of those personal events that many people experience but few speak of it. Other reasons why information about the sound current is so well hidden may surprise you.

Even seasoned teachers of mystic practices are often not familiar with sound current techniques. Most, even if they are aware of the sound current's presence, are not aware of its significance.

Hidden in Plain Sight

I once worked with a revered yoga teacher. Various ringing and buzzing noises plagued one of her students while practicing breathing meditations. The yoga teacher herself had experienced the same phenomenon. Eventually, she was referred to me. She was amazed that she was not familiar with *nada yoga* even after decades of in-depth yoga studies.

I showed her the book *Fundamentals of Yoga*, which was already familiar to her. She was fascinated when I pointed to a discussion of the sound current. The true nature of the topic had not been previously apparent to her. She was even more impressed when she read through the passages with new awareness of the sound current. The author cited the sound current, or nada, as the source of all manifestation and the undisputed pathway to enlightenment. Although this yoga teacher had read the book numerous times before, she had not realized the significance of the passages, or that they referred to internally audible sounds.

This has happened to me many times, even with experienced sound current practitioners. I have had the pleasure of showing them references to the sound current in very unlikely places. They are stunned to realize that many authors are aware of the significance of the sound current but completely cloak their references.

This is a classic example of how information about the sound current is hidden in plain sight. References in the literature are usually brief and obscure by design. An uninitiated reader can pass over these profound statements without realizing what is being discussed.

For someone who has not experienced the sound current, it is a most abstract topic. Even for those with personal experience, the literature usually hovers nearer the realm of mystic poetry and rarely makes definitive statements. Often, a passage seeks an emotional or intuitive response rather than rational clarity, so the language can be highly symbolic.

Most *occult* groups have highly developed internal lexicons specifically designed to elude the understanding of outsiders. They speak and write in a kind of code, partly by design and partly as a result of their own related technical developments. Because these groups function in secrecy, even from each other, they develop unique perspectives and technical vocabularies. Of course, this is true of all groups that delve deeply into a subject, even scientists.

Nada the Word

Everyone has this word but not everyone understands its real meaning. It shines in darkness, in ignorance; but owing to ignorance, man does not understand its omnipresent, omnipotent, and omniscient nature. It is the life and light of the universe.

— Rammurti S. Mishra
*Fundamentals Of Yoga:
A Handbook of Theory
and Application*
p. 133

Occult means "hidden." An occultation in astronomy occurs when one celestial body is hidden from view by another. So, occult practices are simply hidden practices. The word itself does not imply good or bad intent, though both certainly exist.

Knowledge Lives

Modern students of esoteric practices realize that a great deal of previously guarded knowledge is now being widely disseminated. Even so, information about the sound current is still cloistered. It has been such a deeply held secret for so long that it is having trouble finding its way into the public consciousness.

There are people who know a great deal about the sound current. Many individuals and spiritual schools are committed to its study, but this information is still not part of the public domain.

Bear in mind that those communities of spiritual seekers that have guarded their practices involving the sound current consider the sound current to be our most direct and intimate connection with the Source of Creation. It is considered the structuring force of the Cosmos, the most sacred of all issues. For some, its profound nature is reason enough to maintain privacy. For others, including myself, that is the very reason why the information should become public at this pivotal time in our evolution.

Both arguments aside, secrecy has been consciously practiced. I see three motives why groups and individuals have done so.

> ·   Power — *The sound current is considered by many to be the most potent force available to human beings.*

> ·   Greed — *Power corrupts, and many have sought to harness the sound current for personal power over others.*

Mystic Wisdom Revealed

Mystics from Gnosticism, Buddhism, and virtually all religions have come forward with their teachings in recent years. Tibetan monks travel the world chanting and teaching. Most spiritual sects and organizations recognize current times as what the Dalai Lama called "the pivotal generation."

· Karma — *Acquiring karma during one's life is an important issue in many eastern philosophies. Personal liability for one's actions regarding the omnipotent sound current has played a key role in the history of sound current schools. If the idea of your religion is to eradicate personal energy ties with the manifest world, then interacting with other people's direct link to the Source of Creation is definitely not to be taken lightly.*

Because of the perceived serious nature of the sound current by those who have studied it in the past, it has remained largely an occult activity. It has traditionally been taught in a devotional setting, through a student and master relationship, where it has been wrongly perceived that the guru bestowed the sound current on the student.

Unconscious Secrecy

The sound current has been guarded throughout human history just as all objects of power have been similarly guarded and coveted. There are, however, other reasons why the information available is so inadequate. Some are unintentional. One reason for the deficiency of practical information lies in the methods and philosophies of eastern teaching, which until recently was the main source of information about the sound current.

In many eastern esoteric practices, there is a tremendous emphasis on emulating the teacher. Students learn through a kind of osmosis, by emulating their instructors. Lessons are often

Karma is the idea that individuals acquire energetic ties with life as they interact with it. In fact, physics supports this concept, in that all matter is ultimately only energy interacting. Everything has a unique energy signature. Energy cannot be created or destroyed; it only changes forms. That means everything interacts by exchanging energy and that the resonate memory of energy in a given form will attract its past connections. The result is energy karma.

Acquiring Karma

Only actions done in God bind not the soul of a man.
— *The Upanishads*

transferred in a devotional setting, meaning the students devote themselves to the teacher. This ensures the absolute attention and dedication of the pupils.

Devotional teaching formats forge a tremendous bond between student and master, allowing for very intense interactions. These methods also tend to circumvent skeptical review by the student so the student becomes dependent on the teacher. This can lead to stagnation in personal evolution and can be highly unsatisfying to the rational side of the student's nature.

My teacher broke from this tradition. I feel, as he did, that devotional ties are destructive to the student and the teacher. I tell students that they should only give total devotion to their inner Self and highest Source. Their highest available guidance on a conscious level may come from a physical teacher, but that will not last long on a good spiritual path.

Eventually, students become their own teachers. They establish a clear link between themselves and Source. Inner Silent Knowledge becomes their guide. This has certainly been my experience in my own practice of sound current techniques.

Western Wisdom

Inscribed at the dawn of Greek history:

Know Thyself
— The Temple of Apollo at Delphi

Eastern Versus Western Modes of Learning

Devotional practices are one reason why eastern wisdom frequently does not translate correctly into western society. Traditional devotional learning systems conflict with western values. We of the West have been instilled with a high regard for ourselves and others as individuals. Total devotion to another person, to the exclusion of ourselves, is threatening to many Westerners who seek to "know thyself." Easterners frequently put less emphasis on the importance of one's ego in favor of Source.

These differing philosophical perspectives illustrate two main lines of spiritual development and create communication gaps. One school of thought emphasizes an inner journey of self-discovery, while the other promotes an outer union with our Source.

I view both pursuits as mirrors of one another. The inner is the microcosm of the outer and the outer is the macrocosm of the inner. Each is a journey into the paradoxical nature of Being. The sound current, because it lies on both paths, can be used to resolve this apparent conflict.

Eastern Versus Western Modes of Thinking

Because of the paradoxical nature of existence, eastern concepts are frequently misunderstood by western minds. Eastern philosophies often say that we are one with the Cosmos. It is often said that the highest goal is total dissolution of personal ego. That is frequently translated as total disregard for one's self.

René Descartes, the father of modern western philosophy said, "I think, therefore, I am." Most Westerners agree that they undeniably exist. Each of us may be one with everything, but we consider ourselves as individuals to be a valid part of the whole. An apparent conflict arises between the emphasis on the individual versus the whole. Denial of self seems to imply a denial of a part of the whole.

The trouble is not so much in the intent of the eastern statements as in the way rational western minds attempt to translate the paradoxes, to say nothing of the outrageous mystical experiences associated with those paradoxes.

Self Versus self

The eastern idea of extinguishing one's self grates on the western palate. It does not translate accurately into our concept of self. The discrepancy is between the western focus on the conscious personality and the greater domain of the aware Self. The Self with a capital "S" includes all that we are as beings, both consciously and subconsciously. Freud has made us leery of the subconscious as a hiding place for personal demons, but in the East, the integrated intuitive Self is highly regarded. When they speak of losing the self they are referring to our common ego or petty side, not our existence as aware beings.

The issue is not one of who is right, but of true communication. There is a communication barrier between East and West. It is more than a language barrier. It requires a paradigm shift to move between the two worlds of thought. Eastern thought is more holistic, whereas Westerners tend to be more deterministic. The East and West have different worldviews and concepts of Self/self. This only adds to the confusion whenever any nonlinear, intuitive knowledge concerning the sound current, or any other mystic experience, is translated into linear, rational western terms.

Two Paradigms

Ancient, intuitive eastern systems of teaching evolved in technologically primitive cultures. Their external, physical worlds were totally outside the grasp of their scientific concepts. Those mystic pioneers lacked the insights available to modern peoples. The unseen forces of nature, which in our modern world are governed by the principles of quantum mechanics and psychobiology, were explained and understood through superstitions or in terms relating to their intuitive awareness of the Cosmos.

West Interprets East

I had been occupied with the investigation of the processes of the collective unconscious.... [My results] not only lay far beyond everything known to 'academic' psychology but also overstepped the borders of medical, strictly personal, psychology.

— C. G. Jung

In his commentary for

— Richard Wilhelm

The Secret Of The Golden Flower: A Chinese Book of Life

p. xiii

Now, as then, the domain of human perception is governed by enormous complexities. While trial and error was also the tool of inner and outer exploration in earlier times, scientific models of natural forces were not available as guiding paradigms. With each observation, we recalibrate our modes of perception and our systems of interpretation. For ancient mystics, imagination intertwined with reason and the elaborate nature of human beings as instruments of observation to produce systems of understanding that have been outdated by modern realizations.

This does not mean we should throw away the wisdom of our predecessors. On the contrary, it behooves us to honor their discoveries regarding the sound current and other mystic topics by updating them with our own wisdom. Their insights give us a foothold into a marvelous world.

Western Science

The western world has approached issues of the nature of personal reality with the rational tools of modern science. Not every westernized citizen is completely familiar with the details of modern science, but all are familiar with its resultant technology. It permeates our daily lives. Few people consider turning on an electric light a miracle. This demonstrates the gulf between the modern, western, linear, rational mind and the ancient, eastern, nonlinear, intuitive mystics who created the eastern knowledge base concerning the sound current.

For those intuitive mystics of the past, all things possessed magic. They sensed the awesomeness of a universe in which cause and effect tie everything together on an inconceivable scale. There is always a limit to the known, yet the known is an ever-present gateway into the unknown. The electric light would have been a miracle to them and perhaps it should be part miracle to us.

Rational people isolate chunks of reality and attempt to stringently define them. This approach fosters an apparent clarity by creating an objective world. It puts the known in one box and the unknown in another. Science tells us we live in a non-deterministic universe, which we can never fully describe without simultaneously knowing all things. The light bulb will always be part miracle. Our connection to the Cosmos will always be part mystery. That cosmic-human interface becomes tangible through the sound current.

Approaches to the Sound Current

The archetypal paradox of the difference between the rational and intuitive thought processes is demonstrated in the male and female brains. In the female brain, the right, imaginative hemisphere is well integrated with the rational, left side. This produces whole brain or intuitive thinking. In the male brain, the right-left connection is partially disabled.

During the sixteenth week of pregnancy, while the male embryo is forming, special enzymes destroy part of the *corpus callosum*, which is a nerve bundle carrying communications between the two hemispheres. This partial disablement of the connection between the right and left sides allows for isolated, detailed thinking, but it inhibits whole brain intuitive thought processes. Males are genetically specialized thinkers.

Confusion arises when these two different thought processes try to communicate, whether it is female/male or east/

Freud thought that the symptoms of hysterical patients were the result of repressed psycho-sexual childhood memories. This represents a western view of the linear development of human consciousness.

Jung, originally a student of Freud's, came to believe that the collective unconscious was the wellspring of the human psyche. This illustrates his eastern influences and a more holistic view.

Corpus Callosum is a nerve bundle carrying communications between the brain's two hemispheres. The natural state of the human brain is more like the female's, but during pregnancy this connection is partially destroyed in the male's brain.

west. Traditional eastern schools emphasize intuitive, personal experiential learning. Western culture, in general, emphasizes rational learning. We in the West like explanations and impersonal, empirical evidence, but lack the direct mystical experiences of the Cosmos that we secretly yearn for. The sound current is the gateway to those magical experiences.

Yet, people who have learned through strictly intuitive methods often display a high degree of proficiency at their respective arts without being able to produce a solid rational description of how they accomplish their creative feats. This is a weakness in intuitive teaching methods. It is another reason why knowledge of the sound current is not widespread in the West. The sound current has been considered a personal and mystical experience, which has not easily lent itself to rational explanations.

Traditional eastern practitioners often do not have, and do not seek, rational explanations for their systems of learning. When they do offer written discourse, they tend to wax poetic and appeal to the intuitive nature within us. Hence, a communication gap exists between the sources of traditional, eastern, mystic knowing and western society.

Even long-time western practitioners of sound current meditation lack explanations for much of what they practice. They proceed on faith until results manifest. This intuitive system of learning does not produce a broad overview. It develops no rational model as a point of reference. Because they lack perspective on their practices, participants in these systems are frequently trying to find their way in the dark and encounter unseen barriers to progress.

Specialized Brains

In a very selective way, the left hemisphere of the male brain is coated with a hormonal chemical. The corpus callosum...is also coated with a ten week bath, which will destroy a significant part of those communication links, greatly diminishing the young male's ability to simultaneously mix and coordinate the use of both hemispheres.

— Donald M. Joy
Unfinished Business
(Audio Cassette)

We now have the opportunity to apply our modern science and rational processes to the intuitive experiences of the mystic. Through that process we can build a rational model, which can guide us to higher levels of awareness without requiring decades of dogmatic practice. We can have the best of both worlds.

*Saints and seers of all time have
expressed having heard the
cosmic sounds of Hun (the
masculine) or Om (the feminine)
when in the expanded state of
God consciousness...*

— Norman Paulsen
*The Christ Consciousness:
The Pure Self within You*

Studying The Sound Current

Ancient Wisdom

Another source of confusion in the literature is the variety of names used for the sound current. Different sound current schools originating in diverse cultures have used various names for the same phenomenon. Not all of these names are obvious references to the sound current. As traditional schools merge, expand and move in new directions, new names and phrases appear.

We have already seen the terms audible life stream, nada, and Word used to represent the sound current. The term sound current itself is a recent English translation. In keeping with western traditions, it is a more pragmatic term, which classifies the phenomenon rather than referring to its mystic nature.

Other common references include the ringing radiance and Om. Om, pronounced A-U-M, is believed to be the purest representation of the sound current which can be spoken aloud. This is much more in keeping with eastern ways of speaking about the sound current. Most eastern names allude to its mystic power. By studying these mystic names and uncovering hidden references in the teachings of spiritual schools, we can discover a great deal of information about the sound current and come to realize how pervasive our subject is in mystic literature.

Mystic Roots

Keeping in mind that those who study the sound current usually regard it as the very foundation of existence, one would expect all serious inquirers into the nature of the Cosmos to eventually encounter its ringing radiance. In fact, references of all types abound in the spiritual literature. Mystic explorers from all spiritual traditions refer to various sounds encountered on their journeys.

Music of the Spheres

The most apparent allusions to the sound current in the spiritual literature are simply the many statements about heavenly sounds and music. Mystics, and some musicians, portray earthly music as a mere imitation of celestial music.

Throughout the mystic texts, trumpets, heavenly music and choruses of angelic voices revealed higher mysteries to the prophets of old. These individuals had experiences in altered states of reality. Their conscious minds interpreted the events in the manner in which they were later reported.

Those prophets directly perceived fields of vibrating energy normally outside the human spectrum of consciousness. Resonating fields of streaming harmonics within the sound current can be interpreted as a kind of music. The *music of the spheres* could be regarded as a type of fundamental harmonics within the sound current. In this way, the music of the spheres is also a kind of communication, the songs of our life force, the voices of higher awareness.

Biblical Trumpets

After this I looked, and, behold, a door opened in heaven: and the first voice which I heard was as it were a trumpet talking with me; which said, Come up hither....

— Bible: The New Testament Revelations 4:1

Music Of The Spheres are heavenly sounds heard by mystics and saints while in trances or ecstatic states of conscious awareness.

Voices from Beyond

The voices of discarnate souls and those of heavenly hosts are also often referred to as musical or possessing special qualities. Regardless of one's beliefs about an afterlife, the transition into death can certainly be considered an altered state of consciousness. It is only natural that it receives special attention within mystic communities.

The *Tibetan Book of the Dead* describes the experience of passing between death and the next incarnation. It reports that the soul hears

> "innumerable kinds of musical instruments that fill that entire world-system with music and cause them to vibrate, to quake and tremble, with sounds so mighty as to stun one's brain ...."

Such a powerful account of heavenly music goes beyond most people's daily experience of the sound current. Of course, personal death is beyond most people's common experience. People who have had *near death experiences*, such as momentarily dying on an operating table, often report having heard music or other unworldly sounds. Some remain permanently engulfed in the sound current after such an experience.

The Message Within

One thing is clear in all accounts of the ethereal music of the spheres. It carries a message. The message is usually one of

German Romanticism

...echo from a distant world...the angel's sigh within ourselves.

— Jean Paul

Reincarnation

Energy cannot be destroyed. There are those who believe that if people have not freed themselves from the energetic wheel of karma, their energy will be drawn back into another similar life.

Near Death Experiences

I actually didn't move at all; the tunnel came to me. There was the sound of chimes as the tunnel spiraled toward and then around me. Soon there was nothing to be seen - no crying Sandy, no ambulance attendants trying to jump-start my dead body...

— Dannion Brinkley
Saved By The Light
p. 9

love and a deep sense of personal connection with higher awareness.

One could say of most music that it possesses a mood or emotional quality. However, mystics routinely ascribe something more to the "music" they hear in their *soul journeys*. Heavenly music inspires ecstatic feelings and communicates conceptual information. This accompanying intuitive knowledge seems to arrive at a subconscious, non-rational level. The mystic knows what the message of the "heavenly sounds" is without knowing how the meaning was divined. So it is with the sound current in general.

Some may find this analogy a little crass, but the sound current is similar to compressed computer data. Under compression, data is mathematically compacted into a much smaller storage space. Listening to a computer squeal over a telephone modem may not be awe-inspiring, but it does illustrate the concept of compressed information. Might that also be the case in the mystic's experience of altered states and intuitive understanding of heavenly music? Perhaps the music of the spheres is poetically compressed data about the nature of reality. The conscious mind interprets it as music, but to the subconscious mind it reveals profound information. We may have the natural capacity to intuit various levels of meaning in those unearthly sounds.

The Power Of The Word

The power of the spoken word is frequently regarded in mystic literature. "Power words" come in various forms. For example, many systems of meditation employ *mantras*. A mantra

A **Soul Journey** is the mystic experience of traveling out of normal physical reality and into other worlds.

Raptures In A Shaman's Journey

I became conscious, too, of the most beautiful singing I have ever heard in my life, high-pitched and ethereal, emanating from myriad voices....

— Michael Harner
The Way Of The Shaman
p. 3

Mantras are words or phrases repeated during meditation, often silently within the mind.

is a word or phrase believed to imbue the user with its power or intent. The nature of this power may be considered in the following four ways:

1. The literal meaning of the word or phrase as a self-hypnotic suggestion.

2. The patterns of breath control exhibited during enunciation of a mantra have profound effects on human *biorhythms*.

3. Vibrations established in the body during vocalization can have profound effects on human biology and thought processes.

4. The "magical" intent established by the originators and subsequent users of the mantra.

Is it possible to charge a word with a kind of magic through one's intent? Consider that words have specific intended meanings. Every word has an impact that reflects the intent of its creators and users as feelings or pictures. In this way, all words are power words. Words transmit intent. Just thinking a word creates energy patterns in the thinker and affects his biorhythms.

The spoken word is also vibrating energy traveling through the air. As we speak, those vibrating energy waves travel throughout our bodies. When we speak, we vibrate our larynxes. Speaking vibrates our bodies and the air around us. Each word uttered resonates in the speaker's bones and organs. The vibrations are measurable and can directly affect the body's biological processes. Harmonious sounds can even promote homeostasis and healing in the body.

Biorhythms are energy patterns in the body that can be measured by various devices, e.g., electroencephalograph, blood pressure and heart rate monitors.

Thought Energy

Even a thought creates electrical and biochemical energy patterns in the brain. Thoughts are energy patterns in our minds and bodies that can be recorded with an *EEG*.

EEG

Electroencephalographs produce brain wave readouts to measure electrical activity in the brain. Four main types are distinguished.

Beta: normal, awake
Alpha: relaxed, REM sleep
Theta: meditation, creative hallucinations
Delta: deep meditation and deep sleep

Chanting Mantras

Gregorian and Tibetan chanting produce wavering overtones, which can facilitate trance states.

Holy Grail

Arcane societies from time immemorial have been in search of the lost word. Some claim to have found it.... All agree that there is such a word, and that the discovery of it is vital to spiritual progress.

— Sir Colin Garbett

The Ringing Radiance

p. 67

...there is a quest pursued in Masonry, which is concerned with the loss and recovery of a Word.

— Arthur E. Waite

A New Encyclopedia Of Freemasonry

p. 470

Use of a mantra can also affect the user's brain waves. The brain waves of a meditator using a mantra can resemble states normally induced by deep sleep or hypnosis. Mantras, and words in general, have power.

The OM Mantra

The ancient mantra OM is reputed to be one of the names of God. Pronounced A-U-M, when enunciated properly it begins as a vibration low in the body and moves up through the entire body. The body becomes a resonating chamber from head to toe. Once the body is toned in this way, the practitioner is then ready for the higher perceptions of the "unmanifested Brahman [God]" energy, in other words, the sound current. This ancient, holy mantra is regarded as the verbalized sound closest to the true nature of the sound current. The idea is to begin with an external sound and internalize it more and more until one is listening internally to the sound current.

Of course, many of us find ourselves internally listening to the sound current without any effort at all. Hopefully, most of us are starting to feel blessed by our possibilities after reading about the wonderful qualities inherent in the mysterious sound current.

Golem Myth

Other types of power words abound in the world's rich mythologies. Tales of power words come to us from all cultures. In those timeless myths, crusading knights use magic words as weapons while heroes and wizards use words as keys to unlock magic doors.

In the story of the golem, a rabbi fashioned a man of clay. He brought it to life by writing a sacred Hebrew name on the creature's forehead. That word gave life to what was previously inanimate. Later, when the golem ran amuck, the rabbi erased one letter in the sacred name, changing the inscription to the word for death. The creature immediately perished.

This story out of *Hasidic Judaism* is attributed to a specific historical figure and is widely considered to be a true account among orthodox Jews. It illustrates both the power attributed to words and to the human beings who use them. Similar power is attributed to the sound current and the individuals who understand its use.

Creation Stories

Often in mystical and mythical literature, words have the power to create. Words are the vehicle of creation in many accounts of the creation of the world, or Cosmos.

In the Judean-Christian story of Genesis, God spoke and His intent became manifest. This is very typical of creation stories from all cultures. There is a primal tone, a primal force of vibration, which initiates physical reality.

The New Testament of the Christian Bible reads:

"In the beginning was the Word"
John 1:1

Here, the primal tone, referred to as the Word, is synonymous with the act of creation. Many religions have sought

Hasidic Judaism is a mystic branch of Judaism.

... the number of Kabbalists whose teachings and writings bear the imprint of a strong personality is surprisingly small, one notable exception being the Hasidic movement and its leaders since 1750.

— Gershom Scholem
Major Trends In Jewish Mysticism
p. 10

Judean-Christian Creation:

God said, "Let there be light," and there was light.

— *Bible: Old Testament*

Genesis 1:3

that original tone. In some schools of meditation, the sound current is considered to be that initial tone of creation.

Across The Cultures

We now turn to direct references by authors who were obviously aware of the possibility of a personal connection with what has previously been referred to as an impersonal cosmic force. The idea of a primal tone that is the foundation of existence ripples through many cultures. The following is a brief survey of some terms and their meanings as they apply to the sound current.

Nada Brahma

Nada Brahma

… Nada Brahma is the primal sound, understood as "Brahma-sound," "world sound," or "god-sound."

— Joachim-Ernst Berendt

The World Is Sound: Nada Brahma

p.38

Nada in Sanskrit means "sound" or "word." It is closely related to the term nadi. Nadi refers to a river or rushing stream or rushing sound. It also means "stream of consciousness." You can see from these definitions how closely the concepts of sound and consciousness are interwoven in the Sanskrit language.

Brahma is one of the three main deities of Hinduism. Brahma is analogous to the Father in the Christian trinity: Father, Son and Holy Spirit. Brahma is the All-Creator.

Nada Brahma means the "sound of God." It refers to the primal creative sound. It implies that the world is sound. It is the voice of creation, sound become manifest as matter.

Physics would make the same statement but with a different vocabulary. Sound is vibration. A physicist would say that all things are made up of vibrations. The big bang could be referred to as the primal vibration that initiated the universe.

The "voice" of God is one clear analogy that a scientifically primitive culture could have used to describe the initial vibration that created the world. In the term Nada Brahma we see that analogy coming forward as part profound understanding of vibrational energy and part mysticism.

Ancient Hindus were obviously familiar with the vibrations of the spoken word, as demonstrated by their use of mantras. Hence, the "word" is used in their sacred texts as a primary reference to the primal vibration running throughout existence.

Nada, or primal sound, is a common concept in many cultures. The term Nada Brahma is specifically used in sacred writings in connection with the sound current and its internally audible tones.

Anahata Nadam

In the Vedas, anahata means "unlimited tone." Its root words literally mean "no instrument." Nadam means "sound." The term Anahata Nadam refers to sounds not produced by any instrument. An unlimited vibration, or tone, which is not created by any instrument, may be the best description of the sound current one could find.

Saute Surmad

The Sufi term for the primal tone is Saute Surmad. It means the "tone that fills the cosmos." This demonstrates a direct knowledge of the vibratory nature of the universe and the sound current itself.

Anahata Nadam

Anahata nadam [sound current] is the manifestation of the supreme into perceptual mechanism. When you have real nadam, meditate constantly on it.

— Rammurti S. Mishra
Fundamentals Of Yoga
p. 134

Muslim Wisdom

"This is the source of all manifestation.... The knower of the mystery of sound knows the mystery of the whole universe."

— Sufi Hazrat Inayat Khan

The Word

We saw earlier that science views the world as vibrating energy. Now we have learned that mystics around the world specifically refer to the concept of vibrating sound as the force lying behind creation. The terms Word, Nada Brahma, Anahata Nadam and Saute Surmad illustrate the agreement between mythologies from diverse cultures. They also punctuate the parallel understandings held by both ancient spiritual schools and modern science of vibrating energy and its role as the primal creative force.

The Sound Current And Ecstatic States

The sound current is related to states of awareness. When you perceive something that the collective consciousness does not, then you are in an altered state of consciousness relative to the average person. The mass consciousness is, by definition, the normal state of awareness. Perception of the sound current is still considered an anomaly. By our culture's definitions, perceiving the sound current is paranormal. Such is not the case in mystic or *shamanic* circles.

Carlos Castaneda and Michael Harner are well-published anthropologists who have studied and participated in shamanic practices. Both authors frequently refer to hearing unusual sounds as they shift states of awareness.

Investigation into altered states of consciousness mandates an investigation into the sound current. They are like two sides of the same coin. The sound current is so closely linked to altered states that many who are interested in intentionally altering consciousness consider it their most basic tool. It is seen as a direct method of altering perception.

Heaven On Earth

This yoga of the Word not only points the way to life everlasting, but enables the yogi consciously to start living that life and entering into its beauteous rapture not after death, but here and now.

— Sir Colin Garbett
The Ringing Radiance
p. 12

Shaman is a term first applied to the spiritual leaders and healers of native tribal peoples in the Americas. This definition has been broadened by usage to include anyone studying shamanic-type techniques.

A Word about Drugs and Altered States

Many shamanic traditions use hallucinogens to induce altered states. In doing so, they rely on hundreds of years of experience which is handed down to them through rigid apprenticeships. Even with this rigorous training, there are regular incidents of psychotic breakdown and occasional deaths. The potency and detrimental effects of any hallucinogen on a particular individual is difficult to gauge. Even under the best circumstances, the body and its associated energy systems receive a serious blow. I do not recommend the use of hallucinogens to any spiritual seeker. The sound current is natural, safer and more effective.

Exploring the Greater Reality

Admittedly, no exploration into personal power, or the human psyche in general, is without a potential downside. One could make the same statement about most worthwhile areas of human endeavor. Some may say that delving into the foundations of the human psyche and our personal energy structures is a task best left undone, and that the subconscious is better equipped to handle those extraordinary levels of activity. But it seems that we have a great predilection to explore our surroundings and ourselves. Perhaps it is even our destiny.

The sound current is an integral part of that exploration. We all perceive the sound current on some level. Some choose to consciously pursue it. The study of the sound current is a study of energy and awareness. It can be a valuable asset on your path of personal evolution, as it has been for numerous spiritual schools.

Hallucinogens

They opened you up by stopping your view of the world…. The plants are excellent for that, but very costly. They cause untold damage to the body.

— Carlos Castaneda
Tales of Power
p.243

A thought on spiritual practices:

Better never to begin. Once begun, best to finish.

— Zen Proverb

Sound Current Schools

Many spiritual schools study the sound current. All those of which I am aware consider the sound current to be their principle means of access to higher awareness and further *enlightenment*.

Here is a brief list of sound current disciplines. All of these are devotional schools.

Nada Yoga

Yoga is the practical application of techniques to enhance spiritual awareness. Nada means sound. Nada Yoga is sound meditation. It is a practice directly involved with the sound current. We spoke of using a mantra to focus the mind. This eventually quiets its normal thought processes. In sound current meditation, the ringing sounds become the mantra.

Surat Shabda Yoga

This is the yoga meditation system taught to my teacher by Kirpal Singh. My teacher took it out of its traditional devotional framework and altered it considerably. Even in its earlier forms, Surat Shabda Yoga was less stern as a discipline than other yoga systems. It is considered a natural path, not requiring extreme asceticism. On this path, one listens to the sound current to cleanse karma and be shown the way to vertical ascension.

Sant Mat

Sant Mat is Sanskrit for the "Saint's Path." Followers of Sant Mat, also called the "Way of the Masters," view their devotional practices as a science. Students follow prescribed procedures. The sound current provides the pathway, but specific

---

Enlightenment, in general, is a process of acquiring greater awareness. A critical mass of energy can be achieved which suddenly shifts a person onto a new plateau of perception. The term "sudden enlightenment" refers to such significant shifts in consciousness.

The Holy Path of Surat Shabd Yoga

The references to Light and Sound, say the Masters of the Surat Shabda Yoga, are not figurative but literal, referring not to the outer illuminations or sounds of this world, but to inner transcendental ones.

— Kirpal Singh

As compiled by

— Ruth Seader

The Teachings Of Kirpal Singh

Volume I

p.31

saints and sounds are invoked to determine the final destination. Sant Mat is a very structured spiritual program. In this well-mapped view of the Cosmos, everyone is expected to reach the same objectives.

A Word about Spiritual Paths

Personal development is highly systematized in many schools. Strict protocols ensure standardized results, but too much coercion confines individual results. Students try to achieve the prescribed goals and may lose personal expression. The reality of the teacher becomes the reality of the student. Dogma containing specific symbols and formulae for achieving predetermined states of awareness can hinder the individual's own nature and personal journey. This inhibits students at the more advanced levels where personal inner strength and expression become keys to advancement.

Devotional schools tend to fix esoteric states of awareness in objective terms. As we have seen in our brief foray into science, even physical reality is not a completely objective experience. Personal growth is difficult when one's subjective, inner symbols must be revealed and interpreted within someone else's restrictive format.

Balancing Intuition And Reason

Traditional schools rely on close, prolonged contact with the teacher and decades of personal trial and error practice. A rational model provides an overview and direction in one's intuitive pursuits. It is like standing on the bank of a swift river. You look downstream and make your plan. Then you jump in and let your instincts guide you, until you pause again on some distant shore.

Current Times

We have been discussing ancient systems of learning, but it is interesting to note that contemporary authors often refer to phenomena associated with the sound current. These authors have obviously encountered the sound current. They describe various manifestations, but few seem familiar with its true significance.

All those who explore beyond the realm of normal perception eventually experience the sound current. It is natural that books about paranormal experiences make references to unusual sounds. Read any book involving altered states, where topics can range from shamanism to UFO encounters, and there will most likely be an inadvertent comment about inexplicable sounds or pressure over the ears.

Why are So Many Experiencing the Sound Current Now ?

The energy of our times is very different from those of preceding centuries. The nature of our world has changed considerably in recent times. Science has radically broadened our conceptual landscape and altered our physical environment. Along with this, the knowledge of numerous spiritual traditions has recently entered the public domain. Many people believe that the spiritual energy of the earth is approaching a kind of critical mass. This presents tremendous opportunities for human evolution during the next few years.

Earth's Resonance Frequency, or internal cavitations, are reputedly increasing dramatically. This would mean that the planet itself is shifting frequency.

Heightened awareness of the sound current is an indication of these accelerating energy shifts. Accelerated energy is evident all around us. We speed about in cars and airplanes and routinely communicate across the globe. These energy shifts will continue to accelerate whether we are ready or not.

11:11 is another term pertaining to the accelerating energy of our times. This particular reference is to energy believed to have extraterrestrial origins.

It is better to be ready. Humanity can utilize this energy to facilitate great positive changes, but we must be informed. There are many forces involved. New paradigms are required. The degree of our success will depend on our intent and levels of awareness. Studying the sound current can vastly improve our chances.

Although perception of the sound current is still considered an anomaly, in the next few years it will become part of the normal accelerated state of awareness.

*...Aum, the Word or Holy
Ghost; invisible divine power,
the only doer, the sole causative
and activating force that upholds
all creation through vibration.*

— Paramhansa Yogananda

CHAPTER TEN

Beginning Sound Current Techniques

The Path to Spirit

Practical experience is the great teacher. It gives you the opportunity to confirm conceptual learning. Through direct experience, your knowledge acquires substance. This chapter is about gaining a practical relationship with the sound current.

It is natural to seek communion with the sound current. As people seek vital life experiences, they are drawn to its energy. Energy is vitality and enhances awareness. The sound current is primal energy. It is a path to awareness, because it is the echo of awareness itself.

A Question Of Wisdom

As I have discussed, knowledge of the sound current has been zealously guarded. The general population, it was felt, did not possess the wisdom to endeavor on a journey into the structure of the Cosmos. But the larger Cosmos is a reflection of your inner being. Journeying into the macrocosm with the sound current is an exploration of Self. You are a microcosm of the greater reality. You are more than a passive observer. You are an integral part of the Cosmos. You have everything you need for the journey. It is your divine heritage. Trust in your connection to Infinite Knowledge. Become your own guide through the sound current.

Hindu Scripture

Sri Krishna: *You have heard the intellectual explanations of Sankhya, Arjuna; now listen to the principles of yoga. By practicing these you can break through the bonds of karma. On this path nothing is wasted, and there is no failure. Even a little effort toward spiritual awareness will protect you from the greatest fear.*

— *The Bhagavad Gita*
Eknath Easwaran,
Translator
p. 65

Inner Light

Light…light, visible reminder of invisible light.

— T. S. Eliot

The sound current is a gateway to enlightenment. It is also the foundation of reality, the primal tone of creation. It holds limitless power.

When is a person wise enough to bathe in such power? Maybe never. Sometimes you must begin on faith and proceed to wisdom. Wisdom comes through experience. You must allow yourself to wade into the water before you can learn to swim.

Cosmic Key

We are mystical beings who reside in the greater mystery of the Cosmos. In order to touch the unfathomable secrets of the Cosmos through the sound current, we must first possess the inner silence required to truly hear the sound current. A quiet mind automatically precipitates heightened awareness.

Normally, our minds continuously maintain an internal dialogue. This self-hypnotic litany sustains our everyday worldview. All of our energy is tied up and slowly consumed in this mind loop. That determined effort blocks any information not pertinent to the common reality. Valuable opportunities are lost.

Those missed pathways may contain the keys to the nature of the Cosmos. A quiet mind, not expending itself to maintain the normal collection of thought patterns, opens onto new vistas of perception. The accompanying heightened flow of energy and awareness is what we seek to tap into through sound current meditation.

Sound current meditation gives access to levels of energy that are outside of normal perception. The sound current may be regarded as an inroad to vast fields of awareness. Becoming familiar with the tonal qualities of the various inroads provides us with an energy map of the Cosmos. States of consciousness then obtain a kind of relative position with respect to each other. Specific states can then be intentionally located and achieved. Shifting energy and awareness becomes more of a science with the sound current to guide you.

Beginning Thoughts

The sound current is our energy link with existence. It is the information flow that establishes our personal reality. All things are connected through this energy. That flow may be referred to as our connection with *Spirit*. Through Spirit, we are connected to all other energy fields. Spirit also connects us to the one unbroken, unifying energy field, which I call *Source*.

The sound current is more than a connection to energy and its power. It is a connection to living awareness. Spirit is self-aware energy. To handle this type of energy, your mind and emotions must be clear, but do not feel that your thoughts and actions must be perfect. Spirit responds to your intent, but It also knows your inner needs. It will guide you toward your highest path.

Cosmic Trinity

Spirit is the energy flow of the Cosmos, connecting All That Is.

Source is the Totality of All That Is, the most complete manifestation of Spirit.

Self is our unique expression of Source through Spirit, a manifestation of our alignment with All That Is.

Obi-Wan: *Remember, a Jedi can feel the Force flowing through him.*

Luke: *You mean it controls your actions.*

Obi-Wan: *Partially, but it also obeys your commands.*

— George Lucas
Star Wars

Beginning Instructions

Meditation is about letting energy flow. It is not strictly concentration. The problem is that we are accustomed to narrowly concentrating our mental energy to accomplish tasks performed in the world. We are used to <u>doing</u> things. Meditation is a <u>not-doing</u>. It is relaxing into power through listening, rather than grabbing and manipulating.

Exercise
Shifting Awareness

Chakras are energy vortexes that broadcast energy about us and receive energy from others and the environment.

Sitting comfortably, lightly touch your forehead just above and between your eyebrows. This area is called the "third eye *chakra*." With eyes closed, move your awareness to that point. Allow several seconds to get the feel of being there. Now, move your hand to the back of your head. Touch lightly on the knob at the back of your head, which is opposite your third eye chakra. This new area is called the "willpower" because it is the source of your personal will. With eyes closed, send your awareness to this new point. Get the feel of being there. Next, repeat this exercise without your finger, using only your awareness. Then move your awareness to the center of your head. From there, move back in your head until you find a natural resting place for your awareness. This will be the place from which you will do your beginning meditation techniques.

The object of meditation is not to become relaxed and lose consciousness, as in sleep. Meditation is a balanced state of super-consciousness where the normal internal dialogue of the mind is suspended. That dialogue is what holds us in normal, linear thought processes.

Internal dialogue is like a continuously cycling, hypnotic suggestion. With it, we are constantly programming ourselves to think and judge everything as we have been taught throughout our lives. We hold the normal world in place through a form of self-hypnosis. We are incessantly repeating instructions to ourselves about how things should be and what to do next. We are so busy talking to ourselves about what to expect from life, that we are not fully participating in the moment. We are looking in the mirror of self-reflection, rather than at life.

We hold judgments and expectations about life around us. Sometimes we have more than one set of ideas about certain situations. For example, some people might be annoyed by others who are late for appointments, and yet these same people may frequently be late themselves. As easy as it is to see the mistakes of others, it is often difficult to spot inconsistencies in our own mental programming. The mind internally buffers conflicting ideas. Conflicting ideas are rarely loaded into conscious awareness simultaneously. Erratic, inconsistent or schizophrenic behavior is usually far more apparent to impartial observers than it is to the perpetrator or his *codependents*.

Codependents are the people around us who allow, or even facilitate, our conflicting behaviors.

The first object of meditation is to quiet the mind so that it can begin to unravel conflicting thought patterns, freeing up mental and emotional energy. Greater thought energy means higher awareness. Less internal conflict promotes efficiency and peace of mind. To achieve this, we must establish a suitable environment and use some basic techniques.

Sacred Space

The outer environment is important. It must be safe and conducive to relaxation and communion with Spirit. Find a private space where you will not be disturbed for twenty minutes. Turn off the telephone ringer. Make sure everyone knows this is your private time. Children and pets are sensitive to energy. When your energy begins moving, they often want to hop in your lap.

Be still, and know that I am God
— Bible: Old Testament
Psalms 46:10

Once you have established your space, voice your intent. Remember, words have power. Say out loud, "I declare this sacred space where I can meditate in complete safety," or simply, "Clear, Vital Space."

Assume a Joyful Attitude

Positive Thoughts

It is better not to pray than to pray with an angry heart.

— Buddhist Proverb

In the realm of pure energy, thoughts have the power to create. Negative thoughts and emotions charge your intentions with a destructive quality. Positive thoughts and emotions create positive results. Be positive and light in your intent. Put thoughts of daily affairs out of your mind. Choose to be happy in this private time regardless of outer circumstances. Of course, you must be practical. If something physical demands your attention, like the house is on fire, by all means tend to the business of the normal world.

Eastern Energy

It is generally valuable to face true east while meditating. True geographic north can be different from magnetic north. To find true east, you must correct your compass reading for magnetic declination in your specific area.

Exercise
Inner Smile

The quickest way to achieve happiness is to realize you have the choice. Let go of daily affairs. Choose to be happy. Smile. It is almost impossible to have a negative thought with a smile on your face. Smile and feel the light energy it generates. Let that joyful light spread into your chest. Meditate from this joyful space.

Exercise

Body Posture

The easiest way for most Westerners to meditate is sitting upright on a comfortable chair. The most important thing (unless physically impossible) is to maintain a straight, vertical spine. Do not slouch back in the chair. Your head and shoulders should be effortlessly suspended directly above your pelvis. A small cushion under your buttocks may help you sit up straight. Be relaxed but alive in your body.

Beginners may cross their ankles and rest their feet on the floor. Make a loose fist with each hand. Hold the fist with all but the index fingers. Touch your index fingers to your thumbs. Turn your fists palm up and rest them on your thighs. This position will help you stay focused in your body. Meditation is usually far less beneficial if you space out or fall asleep. Meditation will begin with this posture.

Expectations

The kingdom of heaven is at hand.

— *Bible: New Testament*
Matthew 10:7

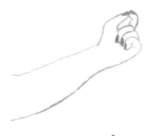

Hand Positions

Mudras help channel energy for specific purposes.

Mudras are hand or body positions that facilitate specific energy flows.

Exercise
Deep Breathing

Relaxing and listening are the two major skills beginners need to acquire. In order to relax, you can use breath as a tool for releasing tension. Close your eyes and take in a deep breath through your nose. Exhale completely through your mouth as you relax shoulders, arms and body. It is sometimes beneficial to sigh or otherwise tone an extended mantra. For example, you could use Oooommmm or Huuummmm. Smile. Let the exhalation's release and the smile's warmth spread through your body and relax and energize you. Repeat this one to three times before each meditation.

Energy Body

The only thing that affects our body is the level and kind of energy to which it is exposed. If we view the body as energy and consider everything that affects the body according to an energy model, we begin to understand....

— Rosalyn L. Bruyere

Wheels Of Light: A Study of the Chakras

Volume I

p. 62

Relaxing while energizing may sound like a contradiction, but that is the idea of meditation. We are seeking a natural, relaxed, vital state of consciousness. Normally, we associate vitality with tension or action. In meditation, we acquire both relaxation and vitality by balancing mind, body and energy. Relaxation allows energy to flow without resistance. A big part of relaxing the body involves quieting the mind.

Mantras

The best way to quiet the mind is by giving it something to do. Mantras are repeated suggestions to the mind. They give the mind a chore and your intent a direction. Mantras should be less than fifteen syllables. Anything more complicated may engage thought processes. Here are some examples.

Everything Is Energy

I Am Higher Awareness

Relax, Breathe, Connect With Sound Current

I Am One With My Source

I Am Divine Light

Chakra

The chakras are seen to be an intermediary for energy transfer and conversion between two neighboring dimensions of being, as well as a center facilitating the energy conversion between a body and its corresponding mind. As chakras are activated and awakened, man not only becomes aware of the higher realms of existence, but also gains power to enter those realms, and then, in turn, to support and give life to the lower dimensions.

— Hiroshi Motoyama
Theories Of The Chakras: Bridge to Higher Consciousness

p. 23

You may prefer one of your own. Repeat your mantra silently to yourself during meditation. Use a slow, even cadence. Following the rhythm of your breath may be beneficial.

When your mind becomes quiet, one of the first things it may attempt to do is run through its backlog of unfinished business. Unprocessed data such as your shopping list and everything else imaginable will surface. As you find yourself engaged in thought rather than following your mantra, simply let go of the thought as if you were releasing a butterfly from one hand. Then return your attention to your mantra as if it were sitting on the palm of your other hand. Imagine bringing that mental hand close to your inner vision to study your mantra. Resume your mantra and release all mental images.

Exercise

Mantra Meditation

Time to try it out. Allow yourself twenty minutes for this exercise. Combining all the previous exercises from this chapter, follow this checklist:

1. Create your sacred space, free of telephones and distractions.

2. Declare your sacred, clear, vital space.

3. Assume a comfortable, erect posture with eyes closed.

4. Choose to be positive, use your inner smile.

5. Use your breath to release tension.

6. Move your awareness just behind the center of your head.

7. Begin your mantra silently in your mind.

8. Relax, Listen, Enjoy.

Do not judge yourself harshly when you find you have lapsed into thoughts. The act of judging creates tension and solidifies the situation with negative expectations. Avoid unproductive self-recrimination. Simply release stray thoughts to unwind their energy. Then gently return to your mantra. This process is quite subtle.

Persevering for twenty minutes should create cessation of habitual thought patterns and allow for moments of peace or even profound awareness. Know that your true nature is sublime. It is only your normal conscious awareness that lives in a rut. You may have to continue for a week or more to release sufficient tension to obtain moments with a completely quiet mind.

Flowing And Fixating

Meditating in the same place, at the same time, every day, helps build a routine pathway for your conscious awareness to access higher realms of energy.

Exercise

Listening to the Sound Current

Mantra meditation is the foundation of sound current meditation. When you are comfortable with that technique, it is time to add the sound current.

The sound current is usually noticed first in the right ear. Right-side tones lead up to higher awareness. This is the easiest and most secure way to begin. Simply listen for the sound in, or near, the right side of your head.

Earplugs

Using earplugs helps screen out external distractions and makes it easier to focus on the sound current.

In time, you will hear buzzing, ringing or roaring sounds. They may come as a feeling or vibration more than a "hearing." You may even perceive the sound current as light. As you listen, you will become more connected with the sound current. It may seem familiar, like something you remember from a long time ago. You may hear many other tones. Listen to the highest, finest vibrating tone. Gently monitor your impressions. Listen to your own inner knowing. Be your own guide.

Exercise
Following the Sound Current

Once you are comfortable with mantra meditation and listening to the sound current, you can begin playing in the tones. Essentially the procedure is to begin with mantra meditation to quiet the mind and enter into a higher state of awareness. When you hear the sound current, listen to it. After you have a good connection with the sound current, begin listening for higher, finer tones on your right side.

When you are listening to a tone on your right side, it may happen that you can hear another higher, finer tone further to the right. Move your attention to that tone. It will lead you higher into the fields of awareness that constitute greater realms of energy and wisdom in the Cosmos and in your own being. Remember, this journey moves simultaneously into inner and outer worlds as you follow the sound current up, back and to the right.

During this process, you usually loose track of your mantra. You are then using the sound current as your mantra.

HIGHER
SOURCE

LEVELS OF
MANIFESTATION

DESCENDING
INTO
MANIFESTATION
ON LEFT SIDE

ASCENDING TO
HIGHER ENERGY
ON RIGHT SIDE

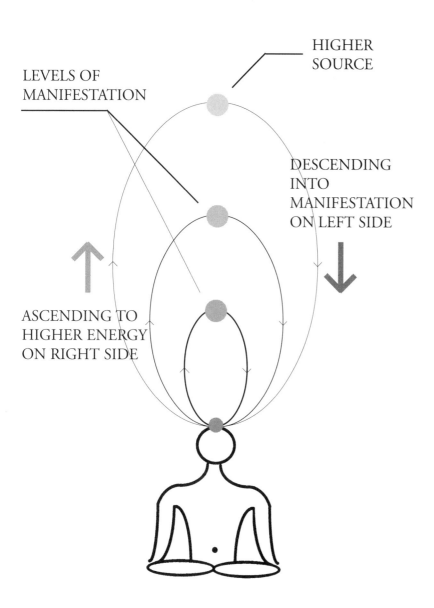

Circulating Field Lines of the Sound Current

Currents of Sound

The sound current is like two rivers of energy. One flows down into manifestation. That is the left-hand side. The other flows upward, back to its Source. Perceived at a distance, these rivers are shining ribbons of light. As your awareness draws closer, you begin to hear the sounds of the rushing waters. You can sit by the river's edge and be soothed and enlightened by sounds from its dancing cataracts. Or you may enter into the stream. There you will be transported. Your Inner Awareness determines the final destination. The ideal path is to learn at the river's edge until your conscious being becomes familiar with the flow. Simply listen at first. Then you can enter. All this is directed by your intent. Proceed like you know how. On some level you do. Spirit will acknowledge your intent and guide you.

Exercise
Entering the Sound Current

Entering the sound current is accomplished by choice, or intent. Focus your attention into it rather than on it. This is a bold maneuver. It can sweep your consciousness away. The securest method is to maintain the focus of your consciousness on the crown of your head. This "crown chakra" is located at your hair swirl just behind the top of your head.

For Left-Brained Engineer Types

Maintain 80% of your conscious awareness in your physical being while 20% follows the sound current.

Allow your spiritual sight to follow the sound current. Think of it as flying a portion of your awareness by remote control from your crown chakra. When your session is complete, return all your thoughts to your physical body.

Exercise
Grounding

Returning to a place of mental clarity, where you can beneficially interact with daily reality, should complete any exercise that alters your state of consciousness. When your twenty minutes are complete, slowly open your eyes. Take a couple of deep breaths. Collect your thoughts. Clapping your hands two or three times in front of your face will focus you. Make sure you are firmly planted in physical reality before you go out into the daily world.

Never do any consciousness-altering exercises when it is not safe to do so. For example, driving a car and trying to shift states of awareness is not a good idea.

Exercise
Spinning-In

This is an energy exercise as opposed to meditation. It is an excellent energy clearing exercise used before meditating and a good grounding exercise after meditating.

Picture a cloud aura of light energy extending out to about arm's length around your body. It is gently swirling clockwise (for most people) around your body. A vertical line of silver-white light just in front of your spine is the center of its rotation.

Imagine a white sheet of clean energy behind you. It is your energy filter. In your mind, bring it forward through your cloud aura. As it passes through you, let it gather all the impurities out of your aura. Clean your filter by shaking the foreign energy away. You may burn it in a white light or release it to Spirit to be recycled for a higher purpose. Then spin your newly cleaned cloud aura into your body. Feel it accelerate its clockwise spin as it draws inward. This vitalizes your consciousness. Do this exercise before and after you meditate. It is also a good way to energize yourself throughout the day.

Meditation Time

Practice this meditation for twenty minutes once or twice daily. Morning and evening are good times. Notable results usually come quickly, but are often followed by plateaus. Persevere. Follow your instincts. Follow your joy. Look for the deeper meaning in situations which distract you from meditation. Exercise discipline when appropriate, but allow your Inner Self to show you new, splendid places.

Spiritual Protocol

Not everything is what it appears to be. Relax and seek the Truth. Think for yourself. Call on higher assistance when needed.

Sound Current Meditation Check List

1. Declare your Sacred Space.

2. Sit comfortably with spine vertical.

3. Position hands and feet, and spin-in.

4. Take a deep breath and relax as you exhale.

5. Let your smile spread throughout your being.

6. Begin your mantra.

7. Find and follow the sound current

8. Lightly return to normal consciousness after 20 minutes.

9. Clap, take a few quick breaths, and spin-in.

10. Carry your inner tranquility into your daily life.

What Should I Expect ?

Good question. The answer is limitless. Expect a quiet, peaceful mind, which remains with you longer and longer throughout the day as you practice. A sense of inner centering will grow. From that place of Inner Silence in your Self, you will be able to flow more easily in all realities and situations, including daily life.

You may see other beings, other worlds, or manifest any number of psychic experiences. These are the worlds of the mystics. Humans are powerful beings. You are in charge. Always use your best judgment. Take command when required. You may call on your own higher awareness for guidance. Be reverent of everything, but do not be overly impressed by anything. Do not be afraid. Listen to your feelings. You are connected to all things. In a very real sense, you are the center of your world. In that place, you are more powerful than anything you may meet in meditation. Trust your inner Self. Spirit will guide you.

Farewell

I have studied with many master teachers. Much of the information I have been exposed to was considered too potent for the general public. All the secret and popularized practices I have studied, and all the other energy techniques with which I am familiar, pale in comparison to sound current techniques.

There is power, wisdom, awareness and great mystery in the sound current. Listening to the sound current will help you become aware of the awareness of the Cosmos. It will also bring Self-awareness. Listening to the sound current is becoming aware of awareness Itself.

You are living in unique times.

Your potential is unlimited.

Farewell and blessings on your journeys.

You may contact us at:

Conscious Living Press, LLC

P. O. Box 50593

Austin, Texas 78763-0593

www.ConsciousLivingPress.com

Communion With The Sound Current

Once the life-stream becomes audible, one is never lonely; for he hears its reverberations at home and abroad. The Voice of God keeps reminding him of the true home of his Father. The practice of Sound Principle rids one of all troubles and afflictions....

— Kirpal Singh

Compiled By

— Ruth Seader

The Teachings Of Kirpal Singh

Volume II

p. 103

Index

By

Subject,

Author

and

Keyword

INDEX

Resource Guide

References

About the Author

Ordering Information

and

Web Sites

Please see our web site for listings
and book purchases:

www.ConsciousLivingPress.com

References

By Author

Austin American-Statesman, A4 January 22
1998
"New Hope for Tinnitus Sufferers"

Joachim-Ernst Berendt
The World Is Sound: Nada Brahma
Destiny Books
1983

Dannion Brinkley
with Paul Perry
Saved By The Light
Harper Paperbacks
A Division of Harper Collins Publishers
1994

Rosalyn L. Bruyere
edited by Jeanne Farrens
*Wheels Of Light: A Study of the Chakras,
Volume I*
Bon Productions
1992, 4th printing

Joseph Campbell
with Bill Moyers,
Betty Sue Flowers
Editor
*Joseph Campbell: The Power of Myth with
Bill Moyers*
Doubleday
1988

Fritjof Capra
The Tao Of Physics
Shambhala Publications Inc.
1975

Carlos Castaneda
The Art Of Dreaming
Harper Collins Publishers
1993

Carlos Castaneda
The Fire From Within
Pocket Books
1985

Carlos Castaneda
Journey To Ixtlan: The Lessons of Don Juan
Pocket Books
1974, 4th printing

Carlos Castaneda
The Power Of Silence:
Further Lessons of Don Juan
Pocket Books
1987

Carlos Castaneda
Tales Of Power
Pocket Books
1974

Wing-Tsit Chan
Translator and Compiler
A Source Book In Chinese Philosophy
Princeton University Press
1963

Deepak Chopra
Perfect Health
Harmony Books
1991

Dr. Quantz Crawford
Methods Of Psychic Development
Llewellyn Publications
1973

Eknath Easwaran
Translator
The Bhagavad Gita
Nilgiri Press
1985, 3rd printing

Dion Fortune
Psychic Self-Defense
Samuel Weiser, Inc.
1996, 4th printing

Sir Colin Garbett
The Ringing Radiance
Radha Soami Satsang Beas
1981, 3rd edition

Michael Green
Discovered and Annotated by
*De Historia Et Veritate Unicornis: On the
History and Truth of the Unicorn*
Running Press Book Publishers
1983

Dr. Susan Gregg
Dance Of Power: A Shamanic Journey
Llewellyn Publications
1993

Michael Harner
The Way Of The Shaman
Harper Collins Publishers
1990

Stephen W. Hawking
A Brief History Of Time
Bantam Books
1990 trade paper edition

Kathlyn Hendricks, Ph.D.
Gay Hendricks, Ph.D.
The Conscious Heart
Bantam Books
1997

Yoel Hoffmann
Translated with Commentary
The Sound Of One Hand
Basic Books, Inc., Publishers
1975

Donald M. Joy
Unfinished Business
Audio Echoes:
A Books on Cassette Series
Vista Media
1989

Christopher S. Kilham
*Inner Power:
Secrets From Tibet and the Orient*
Japan Publications, Inc.
1988

George Lucas
The Empire Strikes Back: Special Edition
Lucas Film, Ltd.
1997

George Lucas
Star Wars: Special Edition
Lucas Film, Ltd.
1997

Juan Mascaro
Translator
The Upanishads
Penguin Books
1965

Rammurti S. Mishra, M.D.
*Fundamentals Of Yoga: A Handbook of
Theory and Application*
Harmony Books
1987 edition

Robert A. Monroe
Journeys Out Of The Body
Anchor Press/Doubleday
1973

Robert A. Monroe
Ultimate Journey
Doubleday
1994

Hiroshi Motoyama
Theories Of The Chakras:
Bridge to Higher Consciousness
Theosophical Publishing House
1984, 2nd edition

Leonard Orr
Sondra Ray
Rebirthing In The New Age
Celestial Arts
1983, revised edition

Norman Paulsen
The Christ Consciousness:
The Pure Self Within
Solar Logos Foundation
1994

James Redfield
The Celestine Prophecy:
An Adventure
Warner Books, Inc.
1993

James Redfield
The Tenth Insight: Holding the Vision
Warner Books
1996

Paul Reps
Compiler
Zen Flesh, Zen Bones: A Collection of Zen
and Pre-Zen Writings
Anchor Books/Doubleday
1989

Jane Roberts
The Nature Of Personal Reality
Bantam Books
1988, 10th printing

Satprem
The Mind Of The Cells
Institute for Evolutionary Research
1985

Gershom G. Scholem
Major Trends In Jewish Mysticism
Schocken Books
1977, 9th printing

Gershom Scholem
Editor
Zohar:
The Book of Splendor
Schocken Books
1978, 10th printing

Ruth Seader
Compiler
The Teachings Of Kirpal Singh:
Three Volumes in One Book
Sawan Kirpal Publications
1985, 2nd edition

Alberto Villoldo
and Erik Jendresen
The Four Winds:
A Shaman's Odyssey into the Amazon
Harper and Row, Publishers
1990

Arthur Edward Waite
A New Encyclopedia Of Freemasonry
Wings Books
1994 edition

Neale Donald Walsch
Conversations With God: Book I
Hampton Roads Publishing Company,
Inc.
1995

Brian L. Weiss, M.D.
Many Lives, Many Masters
A Fireside Book/Simon and Schuster Inc.
1988

Richard Wilhelm
Translated and Explained by
The Secret Of The Golden Flower:
A Chinese Book of Life
A Harvest/HBJ Book
Harcourt Brace Jovanovich
1962, revised and augmented

Fred Alan Wolf
Parallel Universes:
The Search for Other Worlds
Simon and Schuster
1990

Wojciech H. Zurek
Editor
Complexity, Entropy And The Physics Of
Information, Volume VIII
Addison-Wesley Publishing Company
1990

About The Author

Eric Gustafson has pursued a personal spiritual quest for over a quarter of a century. During that time, he has studied esoteric martial arts, including Chi Gung, Kung Fu, Aikido and Tai Chi. He holds a Bachelor of Science degree in physics. He has had extensive training in numerous techniques of meditation and energy use. While acquiring a mastery of Surat Shabd Yoga and sound current meditation, Eric has passed through many amazing journeys. He is now teaching publicly and sharing his knowledge of spiritual evolution. He teaches energy awareness and personal energy management. Much of this information has either long been concealed or is the result of Eric's personal link with Silent Knowledge and his unique blend of science and mysticism.

To Order Additional Copies
Of

The Ringing Sound:
An Introduction to the Sound Current

Order Online At
www.ConsciousLivingPress.com

Or

Mail Payment and Shipping Information

To

Conscious Living Press, LLC
PO Box 50593
Austin, Texas
78763

Make Check Payable to:
Conscious Living Press, LLC

Order Form
Shipping Information

Name _____

Address _____

City _____ State ─ Zip _____

Telephone _____

Email Address _____
   (Optional)

Shipping in USA (except Texas)
$19.95 Premium Soft-bound Cover
Number of Copies ___ x $23.95 = _____
(Includes $4 shipping & handling per copy)

Shipping in Texas
$19.95 Premium Soft-bound Cover
Number of Copies ___ x $25.60 = _____
(Includes $4 s&h plus $1.65 state tax per copy)

For credit card orders complete the following:

Account Number _____

Exp. Date _____

Name on Card _____

Signature